PROJECT

Contemporary
Historical
Examination of
Current
Operations

REPORT

AN OVERVIEW OF INSURGENCY AND COUNTERINSURGENCY IN THAILAND THROUGH 1973 —
A Background Survey for Perspective and a Guide to the Literature (U)
1 JANUARY 1975

CHECO/CORONA HARVEST DIVISION
OPERATIONS ANALYSIS OFFICE
HQ PACAF

Prepared by:
Major Edward B. Hanrahan
Project CHECO 7th AF

DEPARTMENT OF THE AIR FORCE
HEADQUARTERS PACIFIC AIR FORCES
APO SAN FRANCISCO 96553

PROJECT CHECO REPORTS

The counterinsurgency and unconventional warfare environment of Southeast Asia has resulted in the employment of USAF airpower to meet a multitude of requirements. The varied applications of airpower have involved the full spectrum of USAF aerospace vehicles, support equipment, and manpower. As a result, there has been an accumulation of operational data and experiences that, as a priority, must be collected, documented, and analyzed as to current and future impact upon USAF policies, concepts, and doctrine.

Fortunately, the value of collecting and documenting our SEA experiences was recognized at an early date. In 1962, Hq USAF directed CINCPACAF to establish an activity that would be primarily responsive to Air Staff requirements and direction, and would provide timely and analytical studies of USAF combat operations in SEA.

Project CHECO, an acronym for Contemporary Historical Examination of Current Operations, was established to meet this Air Staff requirement. Managed by Hq PACAF, with elements at Hq 7AF and 7/13AF, Project CHECO provides a scholarly, "on-going" historical examination, documentation, and reporting on USAF policies, concepts, and doctrine in PACOM. This CHECO report is part of the overall documentation and examination which is being accomplished. It is an authentic source for an assessment of the effectiveness of USAF airpower in PACOM when used in proper context. The reader must view the study in relation to the events and circumstances at the time of its preparation--recognizing that it was prepared on a contemporary basis which restricted perspective and that the author's research was limited to records available within his local headquarters area.

ROBERT E. HILLER
Asst for Operations Analysis
DCS/Operations and Intelligence

DEPARTMENT OF THE AIR FORCE
HEADQUARTERS PACIFIC AIR FORCES
APO SAN FRANCISCO 96553

REPLY TO
ATTN OF: OA

1 DEC 1975

SUBJECT: Project CHECO Report, An Overview of Insurgency and Counterinsurgency in Thailand Through 1973

TO: SEE DISTRIBUTION PAGE

1. Attached is a Secret document. It should be transported, stored, safeguarded, and accounted for in accordance with applicable security directives. Retain or destroy in accordance with AFR 205-1. Do not return.

2. This letter does not contain classified information and may be declassified if attachment is removed.

FOR THE COMMANDER IN CHIEF

ROBERT E. HILLER
Asst for Operations Analysis
DCS/Operations and Intelligence

1 Atch
Proj CHECO Rprt, An Overview of
Insurgency and Counterinsurgency
in Thailand Through 1973, 1Jan75 (S)

DISTRIBUTION LIST

1. SECRETARY OF THE AIR FORCE

    a. SAF/OI 1
    b. SAF/LLV 1
    c. SAF/US 1

2. HEADQUARTERS USAF

    a. AF/CHO 2

    b. AF/DP 1

    c. AF/IG
        (1) IVOA 1
        (2) SP 1

    d. AF/INYXX 1

    e. AF/LG
        (1) LGTT 1
        (2) LGX 1

    f. AF/NB 1

    g. AF/PRC 1

    h. AF/RD
        (1) RDQ 1
        (2) RDQL 1
        (3) RDQPC 1
        (4) RDR 1

    i. AF/SAMI 1

    j. AF/XO
        (1) XODC 1
        (2) XODD 1
        (3) XODL 1
        (4) XOOG 1
        (5) XOOSLC 1
        (6) XOOSN 1
        (7) XOOSR 1
        (8) XOOSS 1

        (9) XOOSW 1
        (10) XOOSZ 1
        (11) XOXAA 5
        (12) XOXFCM 1

3. MAJOR COMMANDS AND SEPARATE OPERATING AGENCIES

    a. ADC

        (1) ADC/DOT 1

        (2) 25AD/DOI 1

    b. AFIS HEADQUARTERS
        (1) INDOC 1
        (2) INTX 1
        (3) INZA 1

    c. AFSC

        (1) HEADQUARTERS
            (a) HO 1
            (b) XRPA 1

        (2) DIVISIONS
            (a) ASD/RWR 1
            (b) ESD/YWA 1

        (3) CENTERS
            (a) ADTC/CCN 1
            (b) ADTC/DLOSL 1
            (c) RADC/DOT 1

        (4) LABORATORIES
            (a) AFATL/DL 1
            (b) AFFDL/PTS/CDIC . 1

    d. AU - 3825 Acad Svc Gp

        (1) AFSHRC/HOTI 2

        (2) AUL/LSE-69-108 2

e. ATC/DOSPI 1

f. MAC

    (1) HEADQUARTERS
        (a) CSH 1
        (b) DOO 1
        (c) INX 1

    (2) ARRS/DOX 1

    (3) 60MAW/INS 1

g. PACAF

    (1) HEADQUARTERS
        (a) CSH 6
        (b) DC 1
        (c) DOEA 1
        (d) LG 1
        (e) OA 1

    (2) AIR FORCES
        (a) 5AF
            1. CSH 1
            2. DO 1
            3. XP 1
        (b) 13AF/CSH 2

    (3) WINGS
        (a) 8TFW/DON 1
        (b) 18TFW/IN 1
        (c) 51CMPW/DO 3
        (d) 388TFW/DO 1

h. SAC HEADQUARTERS
    (1) HO 1
    (2) IN 1
    (3) LG 1
    (4) NRI 1

i. TAC

    (1) HEADQUARTERS
        (a) DOC 1
        (b) DREA 1
        (c) IN 1
        (d) XPSY 1

    (2) WINGS
        (a) 1SOW/DOI 1
        (b) 23TFW/DOI 1
        (c) 27TFW/IN 1
        (d) 35TFW/IN 1
        (e) 67TRW/DOI 1
        (f) 316TAW/DOX 1
        (g) 317TAW/IN 1
        (h) 366TFW/IN 1

    (3) CENTERS, SCHOOLS
        (a) USAFAGOS/EDAC .. 1
        (b) USAFSOS/ESD 1
        (c) USAFTAWC/IN 1
        (d) USAFTFWC/TA 1

j. USAFA/DFSLB 1

k. USAFE

    (1) HEADQUARTERS
        (a) DOA 1
        (b) DOLO 1
        (c) DOOW 1
        (d) XPX 1

    (2) AIR FORCES
        (a) 3AF/DO 1
        (b) 16AF/DO 1

    (3) WING
        (a) 513TAW/DOI 1

l. USAFSS: AFEWC/SUR 2

4. ADVISORY GROUPS

    a. JUSMAG-Thailand 1

    b. MAAG-China/MGXO 1

5. ALLIED FORCES

    a. Air Deputy - AFNORTH ... 1

6. MILITARY DEPARTMENTS, UNIFIED AND SPECIFIED COMMANDS AND JOINT STAFFS

    a. CINCLANT/CL 1
    b. CINCPAC/J34 1
    c. CINCPACFLT/Code 332 1
    d. CHIEF, NAVAL OPERATIONS 1
    e. COMMANDANT, MARINE CORPS/ABQ 1
    f. COMUSKOREA (ATTN: J-3) 1
    g. COMUSTDC/J3 1
    h. DEPARTMENT OF THE ARMY/ASM-D 1
    i. JOINT CHIEFS OF STAFF/J3RR&A 1
    j. SECRETARY OF DEFENSE/OASD/SA 1
    k. USCINCRED (ATTN: RCJ3) 1

7. DEFENSE/CONTRACTED AGENCIES

    a. Analytic Services, Inc. 1
    b. DMAAC/PR 1

8. SCHOOLS

    a. Senior USAF Rep, Armed Forces Staff College 1
    b. Senior USAF Rep, Industrial College of the Armed Forces 1
    c. Senior USAF Rep, National War College 1
    d. Senior USAF Rep, Naval Amphibious School 1
    e. Senior USAF Rep, USA JFK Cen for Mil Asst 1
    f. Senior USAF Rep, US Army Armor School, Comd and Staff Dept 1
    g. Senior USAF Rep, US Army C&G Staff College 1
    h. Senior USAF Rep, US Army Field Artillery School 1
    i. Senior USAF Rep, US Army Infantry School 1
    j. Senior USAF Rep, US Army War College 1
    k. Senior USAF Rep, US Liaison Office 1
    l. Senior USAF Rep, US Marine Corps Education Center 1
    m. Senior USAF Rep, US Naval War College 1

9. STATE DEPARTMENT AGENCIES

    a. State Department, Washington, D. C. 1
    b. US Consulate, Udorn, Thailand 1
    c. US Embassy, Bangkok, Thailand 2
    d. 51 District OSI, Bangkok, Thailand 1

TABLE OF CONTENTS (U)

	Page
LIST OF FIGURES	ix
ABOUT THE AUTHOR	x
PREFACE	xi

PART A - THE INSURGENCY: ITS SETTING AND GROWTH ... 1

CHAPTER I. INTRODUCTION -- THE INSURGENCY IN THAILAND ... 3

   Historical Sketch of Communist Insurgency in Thailand ... 5

   The Character and Location of the Communist Insurgency in Thailand ... 7

      The Central Region ... 8
      The Northeast Region ... 12
      The North Region ... 12
      The South Region ... 17

CHAPTER II. BACKGROUND TO THE INSURGENCY: THE THAI PEOPLE, THEIR CUSTOMS, AND THEIR COUNTRY ... 21

   The People ... 21

   Cultural Institutions and the Complexities of Society in Thailand ... 29

CHAPTER III. CAUSES OF INVOLVEMENT IN INSURGENCY ... 37

   Regional Discontent and Involvement Among Groups in Thailand ... 37

   Involving the Individual in Communist Insurgency ... 39

      Initial Contacts ... 40
      Developing Relationships ... 41
      Persuasive Propaganda ... 42
      Establishing Commitment ... 43

PART B - COUNTERINSURGENCY: EVOLVING RTG AND US EFFORTS ... 47

CHAPTER IV. THE ROYAL THAI GOVERNMENT'S EFFORTS TO MEET THE THREAT ... 49

   RTG CI Strategy and Approaches ... 51

   Problems and Trends in RTG CI Efforts ... 59

	Page
CHAPTER V. THE ROLE OF THE UNITED STATES IN THAI COUNTER-INSURGENCY	63
US Military Contributions to Thai CI	67
Contributions to Thai CI from Other Mission Components	70
CHAPTER VI. CONCLUSION	75
Epilog	78
APPENDICES	
A. J-2 USMACTHAI/JUSMAGTHAI THAILAND THREAT BRIEF	81
B. IMPORTANT DATES IN THAI HISTORY THROUGH 1963	103
FOOTNOTES	113
BIBLIOGRAPHY	119
GLOSSARY OF ABBREVIATIONS AND ACRONYMS	149
GLOSSARY OF TERMS	155

LIST OF FIGURES (U)

Figure No.		Page
1.	Provinces of Thailand	4
2.	Communist Insurgent Activity in Thailand	9
3.	West Central Thailand	11
4.	Cambodian Border Provinces	13
5.	Northeast Thailand	14
6.	North Thailand	15
7.	Mid-South Thailand	18
8.	Far South Thailand	19
9.	Location and Topography of Thailand	22
10.	Thai Kingdoms, Eighth to Sixteenth Centuries	23
11.	Thai Territory Lost to Britain and France 18th to 20th Centuries	25
12.	Concentrations of Major Ethnic Minorities in Thailand	27
13.	Ethnic Minorities in North Thailand	28
14.	China and Areas Formerly Under Chinese Control	77

ABOUT THE AUTHOR (U)

Major Edward B. Hanrahan, A.B. Columbia College, Columbia University, A.M. and Ph.D. University of Illinois, was an Associate Professor of Geography at the United States Air Force Academy before joining the Project CHECO staff. He has had a long association with Southeast Asia and Thailand, having been assigned to the Philippines and Thailand from August 1961 to June 1963 and having developed Southeast Asia as a regional specialty for his graduate work at the University of Illinois. Upon leaving Project CHECO he assumed duties with the USAF Environmental Technical Application Center, Washington, D.C.

PREFACE (U)

The Air Staff tasked Project CHECO to write continuing reports on counterinsurgency in Thailand. Normally, the first work in a continuing report series describes the overall situation, and subsequent reports provide annual or biannual updates. Underlying details about the Thai insurgency, however, have slowly been coming to light over the past few years, therefore, counterinsurgency has necessarily continued to evolve and past CHECO works on counterinsurgency have been limited to reporting the specific end events of force and counter force.[1] This study attempts to delimit the background to the Thai insurgency and counterinsurgency.

Preliminary surveys of the literature and data available indicated that insurgency and counterinsurgency in Thailand have been well documented but that pertinent information is scattered throughout a multitude of separate reports and studies by many agencies. Consequently, one must read numerous publications to become enlightened on all but the most narrowly focused insurgency/counterinsurgency topics. This report attempts to integrate in one volume for the staff officer a broad background and wide perspective of insurgency and counterinsurgency in Thailand. It extracts from many of the completed works and indicates where more detail can be found.* It avoids duplicating lengthly explanations already published, avoids citing detailed statistics on armed conflict which are all too often misleading indicators, and avoids discussing personalities which have been important but are left to more exhaustive studies. Due to the

---

*See Bibliography, p. 115ff.

the nature of its comprehensive approach, this report only indicates the complexities of the Thai insurgency/counterinsurgency and sketches in broadest terms the cultural heritage of the Thai.

The author is indebted to several offices and many individuals for their assistance in gaining perspective and obtaining data:

- to Maj Gen Thomas W. Mellen and his staff at United States Military Assistance Command/Joint United States Military Advisory Group, Thailand, especially Col Leonard Volet, Maj Kenneth J. Alnwick, and Lt Col Max E. Newman for ideas and critique, and Lt Col John R. Pickett for documents.

- to Counselor William N. Stokes, Mr. Chuck Penney, and the Development and Security Staff at the US Embassy, Bangkok, especially Dr. James L. Woods of the Advanced Research Projects Agency for his data and organization assistance;

- to American Consul Jere Broh-Kahn, Udorn;

- to The Deputy Commander Seventh/Thirteenth Air Force -- Thirteenth Air Force Advanced Echelon Directors of Security Police and Civic Actions; and

- to Mr. P.B.G. Waller of the Stanford Research Institute, Bangkok.

This document was reviewed and approved by the United States Military Assistance Command/Joint United States Military Advisory Group, Thailand, and the United States Embassy in Bangkok, the single US Government manager for all matters relating to Thai insurgency and counterinsurgency.

Udorn, Thailand
January, 1974

PART A -- THE INSURGENCY: ITS SETTING AND GROWTH

STATEMENT OF FIELD MARSHAL THANOM KITTIKACHORN, FORMER PRIME MINISTER ROYAL THAI GOVERNMENT[2]

It is the desire of the Thai people to live at peace with their neighbours and all countries and to enjoy tranquility within the Kingdom. It is the objective of the Royal Thai Government to attain these conditions of peace and tranquility so that the welfare of the Kingdom may be steadily increased through programmes of economic and social development. However, none of this can be possible without the maintenance of Thailand's traditional and cherished freedom and independence. Unfortunately, in recent years it has become apparent that there are some powers which are unwilling to see Thailand at peace. Those powers decline to allow the Royal Thai Government and its people the right to deal themselves with their problems and with the opportunities for progress and change which modern conditions present.

The White Paper which follows* describes the subversive insurgency which has been created in Thailand because of external interference in our domestic affairs. It gives positive evidence of the increasing external support which is given to the Thai Communist insurgents by certain proponents of an ideology foreign to Thailand and which the Government sincerely believes the Thai people have no desire to embrace. The threat posed to Thailand and its beloved institutions is a most grave one for it is ruthlessly pursued with violence and scorn of human life and suffering. It has brought death and destruction to thousands of Thai families and has caused a most serious diversion of Thai resources from the tasks of development to the task of providing security to the people of our countryside.

The people of Thailand did not initiate this struggle. We have no designs upon the territory of other countries, nor do we wish to dictate to them the forms of government and social institutions which they shall have. It is our sincere hope that they will in due course choose to follow the same principles with respect to the Kingdom of Thailand. In the meantime, the world should know that the Thai people, under the leadership of their Government and united in their love for the royal family, the Kingdom of Thailand, and the Buddhist religion shall steadfastly resist this new form of aggression and shall persevere in preserving their independence and institutions in the face of all adversity.

Field Marshal T. Kittikachorn

* The referenced White Paper does not follow herein.

CHAPTER I

INTRODUCTION -- THE INSURGENCY IN THAILAND (U)

(C) Briefly, the insurgency in Thailand is communist controlled, subversive to the Royal Thai Government (RTG), and largely externally supported. The insurgency is ostensibly directed by the Communist Party of Thailand (CPT) and follows traditional Maoist form closely. The Chinese Communist Party (CCP), the Vietnamese Communist Party (Lao Dong), the Lao Communist Party, and the Communist Party of Malaya (CPM) provide varying amounts of political and military assistance. The Chinese appear to have the greatest ideological influence on the insurgency in Thailand. In fact, levels of support, Communist Terrorist (CT) activity, and the insurgency itself appear to be instruments of foreign policy of the Chinese People's Republic (CPR) and to some extent of the Democratic Republic of Vietnam (DRV).[3]

(C) Members of the CPT and the leadership cadre of communist front and CT organizations are native Thai usually trained in China, North Vietnam, or Laos. The insurgency is generally in the organizational stage with ultimate focus on a "war of national liberation," but insurgents in some areas of the North, Northeast, and South have been conducting guerrilla warfare since 1965. In 1973 (2516*) the insurgency continued to grow slowly on a long continuum. The US Government viewed the insurgency as serious, but, practically speaking, RTG officials considered it less than serious.[4]

---

* (U) The year of the Buddhist Era (B.E.). Dates are B.E. in Thai documents which the reader may want to cross-reference.

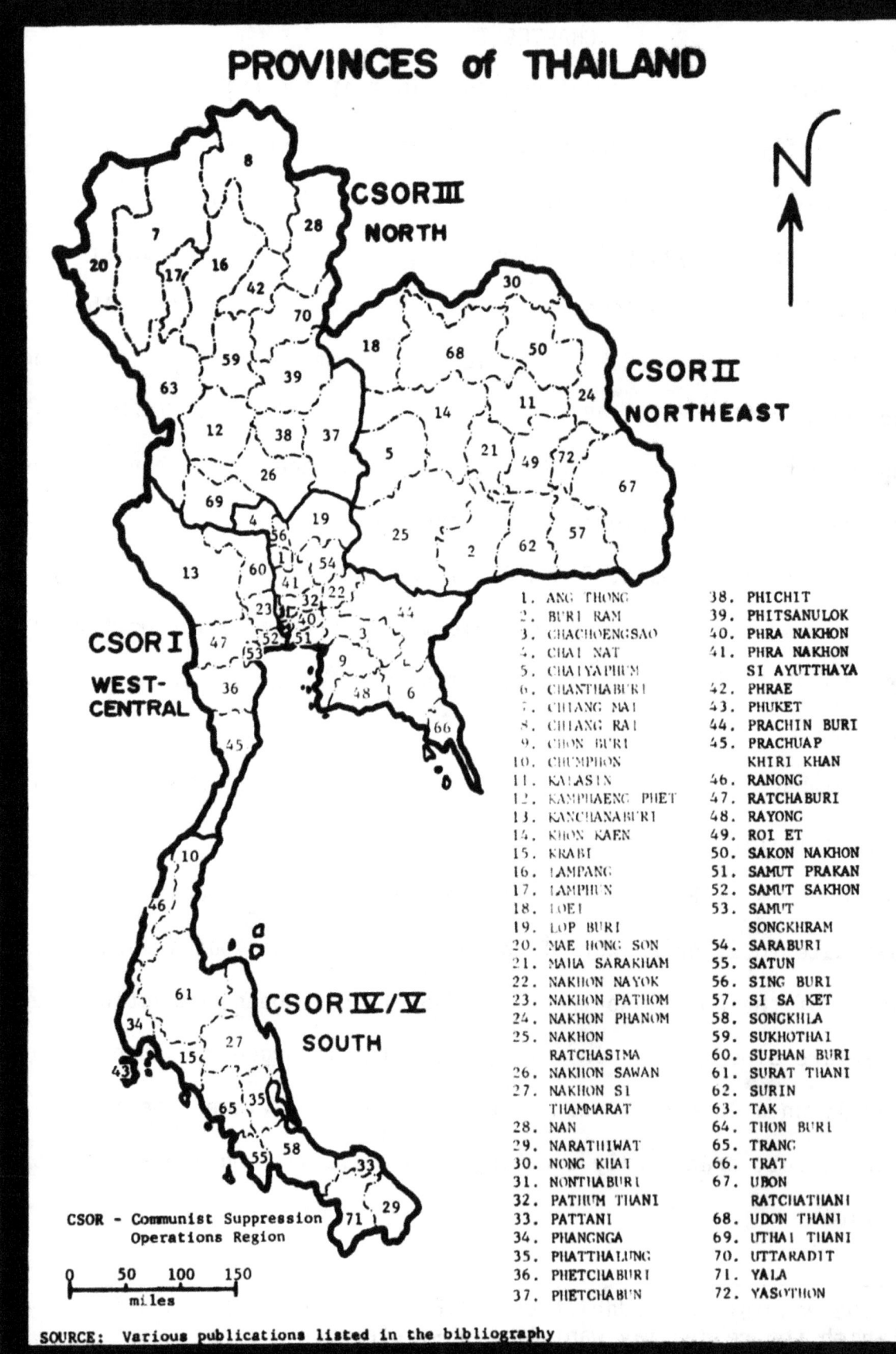

FIGURE 1

Historical Sketch of Communist Insurgency in Thailand (U)

(C) The first recorded communist activities in Thailand were membership recruiting efforts of the CCP among resident Chinese in Thailand during the 1920s. Also in the 1920s the pro-communist Chinese in Thailand, increased by immigration as well as recruiting, organized their own "Thai" groups such as the Communist Youth of Siam and Marxist-Leninist Units. Vietnamese communist organizers started activities in the Northeast during this period and even moved the Lao Dong Headquarters to the Northeast between 1931 and 1933 in order to avoid French suppression in Indochina.[5]

(C) Communist subversive propaganda increased after the constitutional monarchy replaced the absolute monarchy in the Thai Revolution of 1932. During the middle 1930s, the Communist Party of Siam (CPS) had representation at the Seventh Comintern (1935), and the first overt demonstration occurred at Khon Kaen in the Northeast (1936). The CPS (formed sometime between 1929 and 1935) grew during the late 1930s and early 1940s as communist influence increased in Thailand's Chinese community as a result of anti-Japanese feelings emanating from China. Cadres of the CCP entered Thailand in 1942 and convened a meeting of Thai communists composed predominately of ethnic Chinese and Vietnamese, but including a few ethnic Thai from the Northeast. This meeting is considered by present-day Thai communists to be the founding of the Communist Party of Thailand, although the CPS started earlier and the reorganization of the communists in Thailand into the Thai Communist Party (TCP)* and the Chinese Communist Party of Thailand (CCPT)** occurred in 1946.

---

* (U) TCP changed its name to CPT in 1952.
** (U) CCPT subsequently dissolved when the communists gained control of the Chinese mainland.

(C) During World War II (WWII), the CPT was active in the Free Thai movement against the Japanese, and some of the old Free Thai support centers still operate upcountry under the control of the CPT in support of the communist terrorists. The CCPT war assignment was to organize anti-Japanese efforts between Kuomintang and communist factions of the Chinese in Bangkok. The CCPT, however, never officially joined the Free Thai movement. For the remainder of the 1940s, communists in Thailand increased their influence in trade unions, schools, Chinese language press, and similar organizations.

(S) The 1950s saw both a rural and urban expansion of communist influence into student, temple, musical, sports groups, and (especially) labor associations. At the same time, infiltration of political institutions received substantial attention. The CPT formed and developed political and propaganda "front" organizations, and political and propaganda assistance from the CRP grew. A National Minorities Institute for indoctrinating Thai and other ethnic groups from Yunnan Province, China, began operations in Kunming in 1951, while a Thai People's Autonomous Region in Southern Yunnan was created in 1953. Communist activities remained unobtrusive in the Thai urban areas but became increasingly bolder in certain parts of the Thai countryside. The Second Party Congress met in 1952 and increasingly larger numbers of Thai went to China for cadre training during the 1950s.

(C) The Third Party Congress met in 1961 and formally resolved to move to a "revolutionary armed struggle" that would start after the CPT established a village support base. The CPT continued to send increasing numbers of Thai abroad to train as cadres and worked at giving the insurgency an ever-larger ethnic Thai presence. Communist propaganda attacked the RTG corruption and US intentions and war making in Southeast Asia. The primary propaganda medium was the Voice of the People of Thailand which started to broadcast in 1962. The CPT began employing more armed jungle forces (especially after 1964) to discredit the RTG's control and authority in outlying regions and also to respond to growing RTG counterinsurgency (CI) activities. In 1965, the CPT established the "Anti-American Movement in Thailand," (its first armed unit) and began an overt armed struggle with RTG forces. The reason for moving into active guerrilla warfare before securing an extensive, safe base area of support in the village was complex, but it hinged on the Thai involvement in Vietnam and pressure on the CPT from the DRV and the CPR. The "Thai People's Liberation Armed Forces" (RPLAF) that grew out of the 1965 beginnings have been slowly gaining strength and increasing their activities with arms, supplies, and training provided from China, North Vietnam, and neighboring communist areas.

The Character and Location of the Communist Insurgency in Thailand (U)

(C) From the national viewpoint and on theoretical grounds, it is accurate to consider the insurgency in Thailand a single, communist movement. For the practical purposes of understanding the events of the insurgency and evaluating possible counterinsurgency solutions, however, a different view may be more effective -- that of several regional insurgencies in Thailand. Each regional insurgency has some degree of communist involvement and control, but there are significant regional differences in the ethnic backgrounds, the political feelings, and the cultures of the people recruited by the communist organizers. In addition, the terrain, the types of communist appeals, and the logistical support vary regionally. The one aspect that does not vary from one area to the others is the strategy of the recruiting methodology. The communists realize that they have no nationwide issues and instead, maximize local and individual grievances after extensive, low-profile research of the locality and the individual. The strategy is thus to develop whatever tactics are required to recruit in each region.[6]

(U) Several regional schemes are used to subdivide Thailand -- all are variations on a Central, South, North, and Northeast regionalization. (Often included are additional sub-regional distinctions for the West Central, Mid-south, and Far South areas of the country.) The Central Region extends from Burma to Cambodia, and at its heart is the middle and the lower Chao Phraya River valley around Bangkok. The highlands due north from the central valley and lying between Northeastern Burma and Western Laos form the North Region. The Korat Plateau to the northeast of the Central region and lying within the great bend of the Mekong River and Northern Cambodia is called the Northeast Region. The central and southern portions of the Isthmus of Kra constitute the South Region.[7]

(C) <u>The Central Region</u> is the core land of Thailand. It is the land around the northern part of the Gulf of Siam with Bangkok at its center. It has the best roads, the best communications, the richest farm lands, the highest per capita income, and the strongest government control of any region in Thailand. It includes the provinces (changwats) from

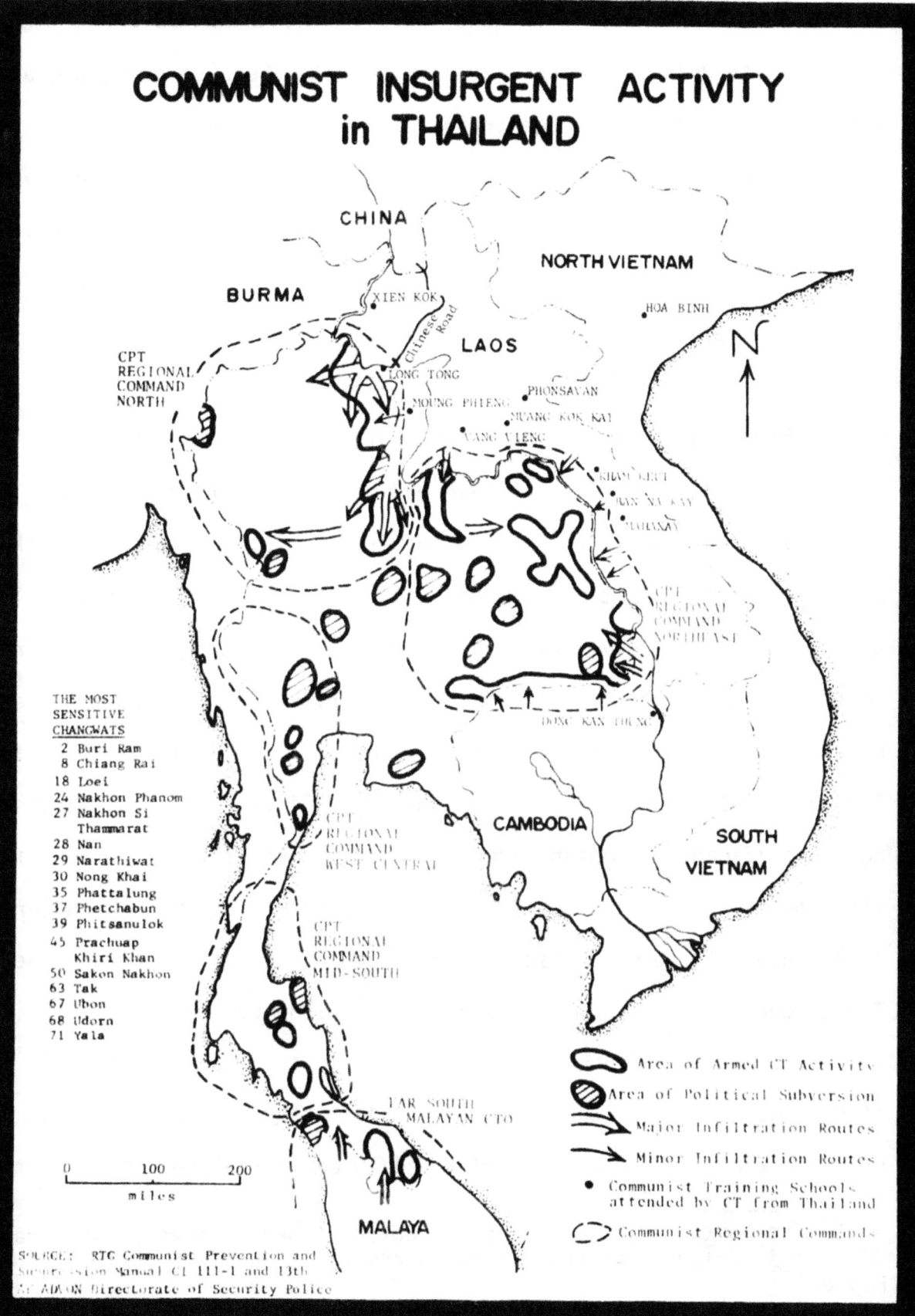

FIGURE 2

Prachuap Khiri Khan north to Kanchana Buri and Khamphang Phet, then east and south to Phichit, Prachin Buri, and Trat. Because of strong and effective RTG control and general prosperity, the center of this area has had few overt communist terrorist incidents. The RTG feels, however, that CPT direction, financing, and overall command and control have been centered in Bangkok, although the CPT leaders are now in the field with the jungle soldiers.

(C) West Central Thailand, especially in the mountains of those provinces bordering on Burma, and East Central Thailand, comprised by the provinces bordering Cambodia, have had more overt CT activities. The incidents in the West Central Region were initially associated with banditry, possibly resulting from dissident factions in an economically depressed area. Today, intelligence estimates attribute current incidents to communist influence bordering on outright control. The Cambodian Border Provinces of Trat, Chanthaburi, and Prachin Buri in the Central Region as well as Korat, Buri Ram, Surin, and Si Sa Ket in the Northeast have significant Cambodian minority groups. The RTG is concerned that the minority populations will become dissatisfied because of cultural differences and be more susceptible to communist recruiting and coercion. The concern is mostly with the potential in the Central Region; to date, Korat, Buri Ram, and Si Sa Ket in the Northeast have been sites of significant incidents near the Cambodian border. The western and eastern edges of the Central Region had 125 to 150 armed CPT controlled insurgents in mid 1972.*

---

* (C) The North Vietnamese Army conducted sapper attacks on American installations at U-Tapao (Central Region), and Ubon and Udorn (both Northeast Region).[8]

FIGURE 3

(C) The Northeast Region has been the "poor country cousin" region of Thailand. It has the poorest roads, the poorest communications, the poorest and driest farmlands, the lowest per capita income, and the least secure and effective central government control of all of the major regions. It includes the provinces of Loei, Chaiyaphum, Korat, and those farther east. The Northeast Region is bordered on the south by Cambodia and on the east and north by Laos. The RTG has feared insurrection in this region more than any other because of the strong affinity of the northeastern Thai for the Thai peoples of neighboring Laos. The Vietnamese refugees and the Cambodian minority are possible supporters of communist activities that are likely to spread rapidly through the economically depressed area at the far reaches of central government control. The RTG has already had some cause for concern with the irredentist movement of Pridi Phanomyong and his followers since 1947, the history of political unrest, the starting of the Thai insurgency in the Northeast in 1961, and the widespread and growing number of CT incidents since then. CT activity has been prevalent in Changwats Nong Kai, Udorn, Khon Kaen, Sakon Nakhon, Nakhon Phanom, Ubon, Buri Ram, Loei, and Kalasin. Fringe areas of Surin, Si Sa Ket, and Roi Et as well as Korat have also been involved. Mid 1972 estimates showed 2,000 full-time armed insurgent soldiers and more than 4,000 village militiamen organized by the CPT in the Northeast.

(C) The North Region includes the provinces of Phetchabun, Phitsanulok, Sukhothai, Tak, and those to the north in the arch formed by Northeastern Burma and Northwestern Laos. The Thai in the North are probably

FIGURE 4

FIGURE 5

FIGURE 6

more culturally involved with the Central Thai than are either the northeasterners or the southerners, and dissent among the ethnic Thai who farm the lowland river valleys is low. The 4,000 to 5,000 armed insurgents under CPT control have been essentially highland tribal people and predominantly Meo with Thai and Sino Thai leadership. Their dissatisfaction centers on cultural issues of land use in the mountains, economic pursuits, and political autonomy. CT incidents have largely been in Nan, Chiang Rai, and Tak provinces and have involved armed bands of hill tribesmen attacking RTG projects and units. While RTG concern has been mostly with the Northeast because of ethnic Thai involvement in the insurgency, the RTG has possibly been more aggressive in the North because of the low involvement of ethnic Thai. The RTG policy in the North has been to bomb and burn the Meo into submission. The results have been to make the Meo insurgents more receptive to communist support and to precipitate a virtual state of war between some Meo tribes and the RTG. The RTG has retreated somewhat toward a policy of containment. In many areas, the insurgent hill tribes in the uplands have been left along while the RTG attempts to consolidate its control in the lowlands. Remaining efforts of government forces in the highlands have shifted toward civic action programs and resettlement of nonhostile tribes to more secure areas.

(C) The insurgency in the North is less clear than in many of the other regions of Thailand because of the opium trade and the presence of Chinese irregular forces. The presence of Kuomintang troops, stranded in the northern Burma-Laos-Thailand areas since the close of the Second

World War and the Chinese Communist takeover of the mainland, has been a mixed blessing. They have been used intermittently during the past 20 years as border guards against Chinese Communist incursions into Burma. The Kuomintang have been active in guarding trade routes and caravans, but, on the other hand, are notorious for their association with opium movements. The Kuomintang troops have also been hired by the RTG to locate and destroy CT forces and base camps in the remote portions of the North. The consensus of the governments of Thailand, Laos, and Burma now leans toward removing the Kuomintang and their disruptive influence on the politically unsettled northern border areas.

(C) <u>The South Region</u> consists of the Kra Isthmus, except for the northernmost provinces of Phetchaburi and Prachuap Khiri Khan which form the western shore of the Bight of Bangkok. Its two subregions are the Mid-south from Chumphon Changwat to Trang and Phattalung and the Far South of Satul, Songkhla, Pattani, Yala, and Narathiwat provinces. Poverty, RTG corruption, official ineptness, and Thai-Malay cultural incompatibilities have been the basic causes of dissention in both sub-regions. The armed units in the South include bandits, Communist Terrorists of the CPT, and the 8th, 10th and 12th regiments of the Communist Terrorist Organization (CTO)*. The CTO is the Malayan Communist Party's armed group which developed its safehavens just inside the Thai border after the start of active suppression operations in Malaya by the British during the 1950s. The CTO is active in Malaya and usually has clashed with RTG forces when inadvertently surprised during chance

---
* Possibly the 5th Regiment also.

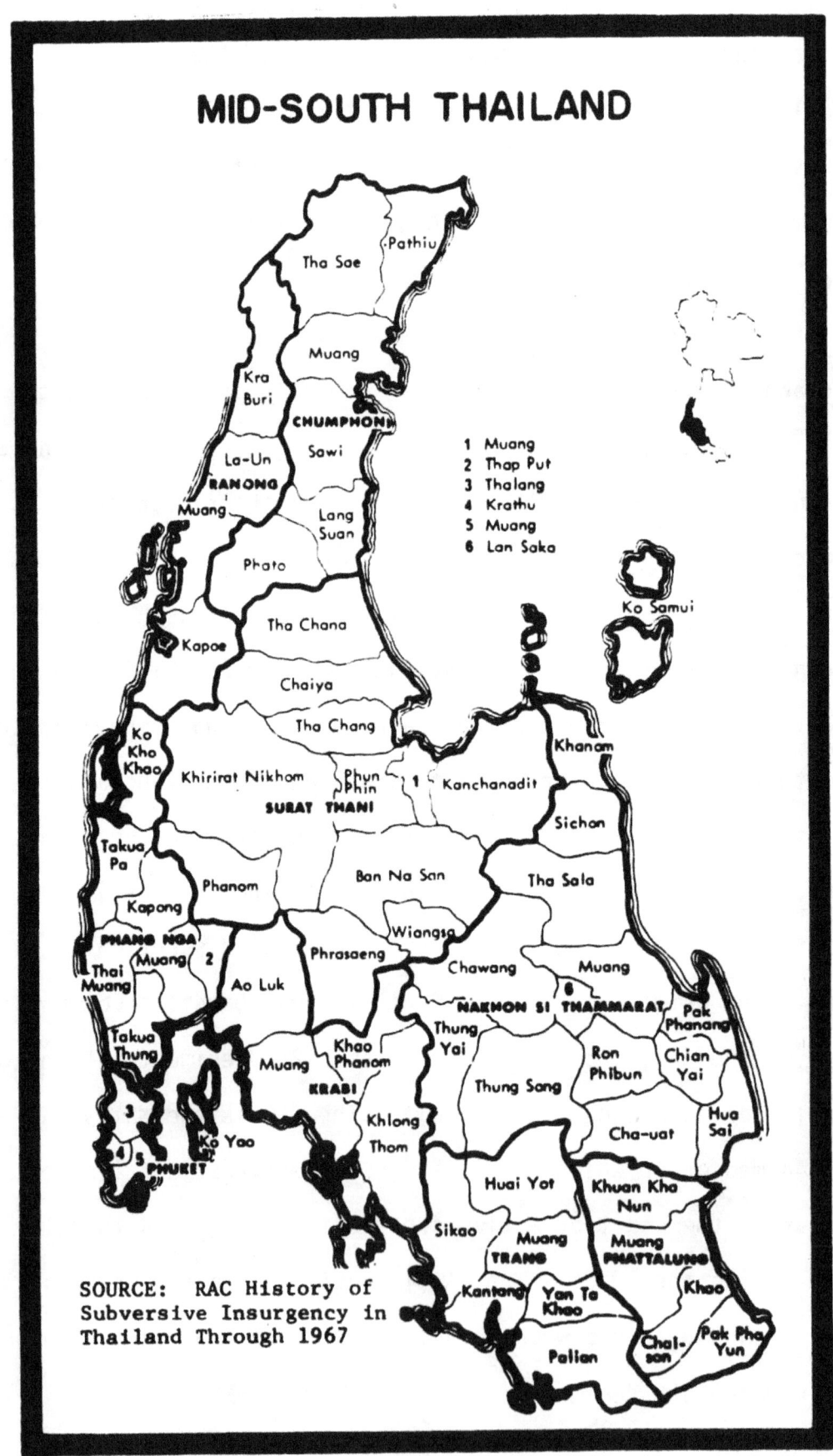

FIGURE 7

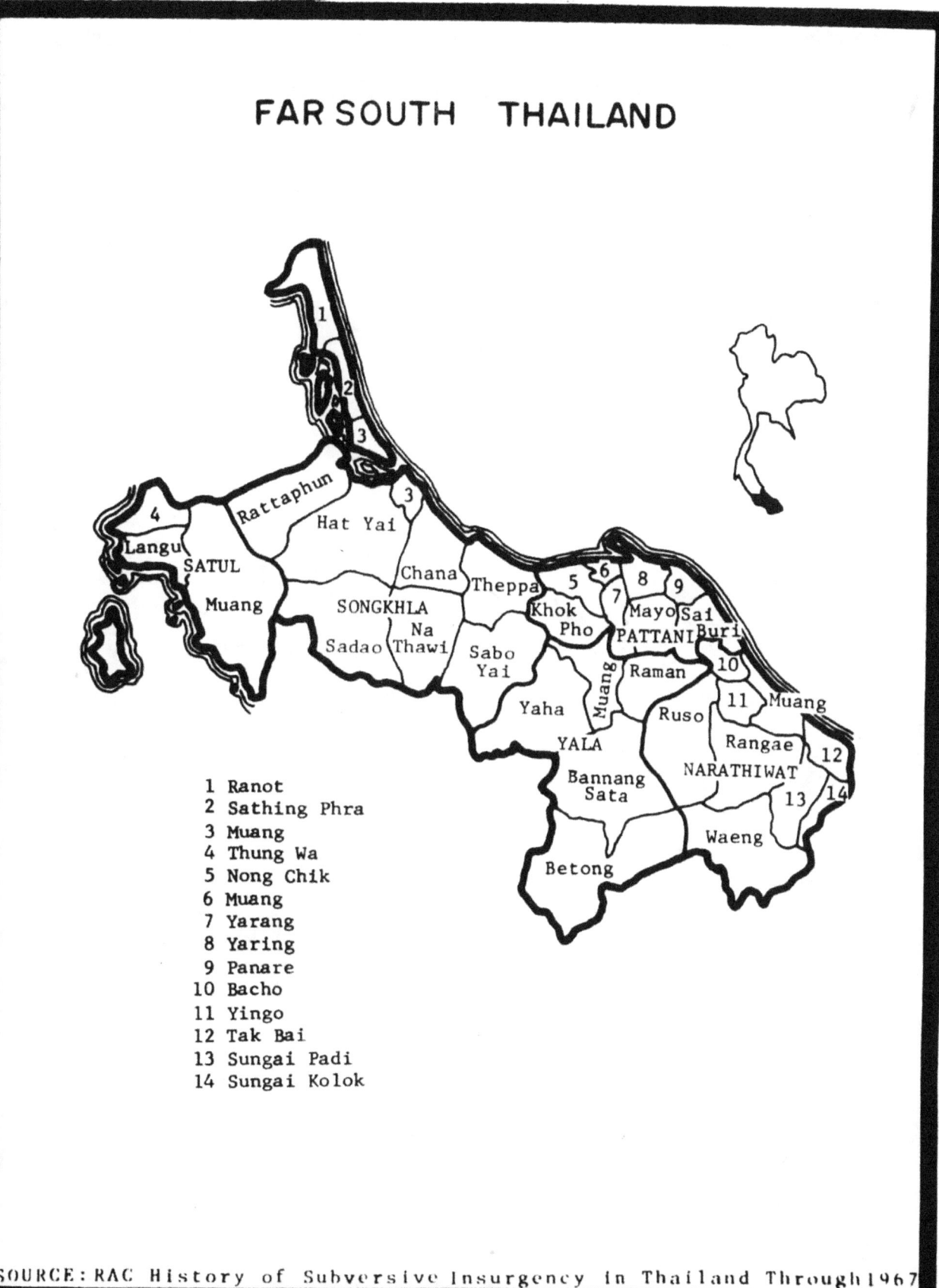

FIGURE 8

meetings. It is not currently a direct threat to the RTG, although joint Thai-Malay government forces have operated in the Far South to suppress CTO activities and destroy CTO forces.

CHAPTER II

BACKGROUND TO THE INSURGENCY: THE THAI PEOPLE, THEIR CUSTOMS, AND THEIR COUNTRY (U)

(U) The westerner only sees a part of Thai culture and seldom comprehends the part that he does see. The reason for difficulties of perception and comprehension goes beyond the westerner's lack of many common experiences with the oriental. The cultures of the Thai people and their neighbors have not only developed different ways of doing things, but have also instilled in the various peoples very rigid ways of looking at life, thinking, and perceiving events. (Obviously, this is true of any culture.) An American looking at the Thai and Thai events through the lenses of his American cultural value system is not apt to understand the Thai insurgency/counterinsurgency (I/CI) and is less likely to offer realistic critiques and solutions. A few words on Thai heritage and culture may help provide more insight into both the Thai insurgency and the counterinsurgency.[9]

The People (U)

(U) Over hundreds of years, the Thai migrated from the Lake Tali region of northwest Yunnan Province, China, with the major migration ocurring during the middle of the 13th Century after the Mongol armies of Kublai Khan defeated Nan Chao. This ancestral homeland of the Thai on the Tibet side of Southern China lay astride the upper reaches of the Salween, Mekong, and Song Koi (Red) Rivers. As the Thai Kingdom of Nan Chao developed in Yunnan from the 6th to 13th Centuries, Thai were migrating down the river valleys toward the Bay of Bengal, the Gulf of Tonkin, and

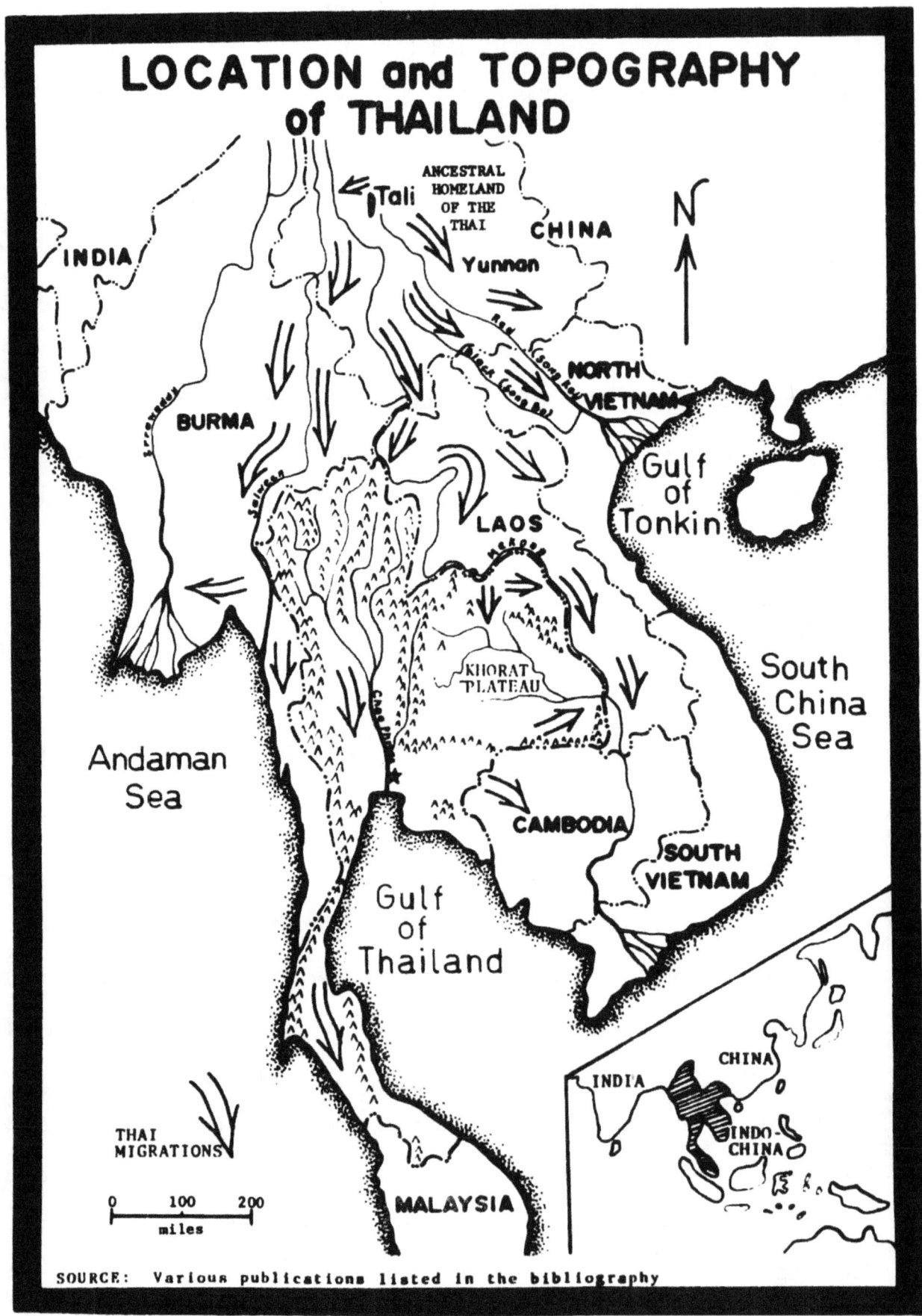

FIGURE 9

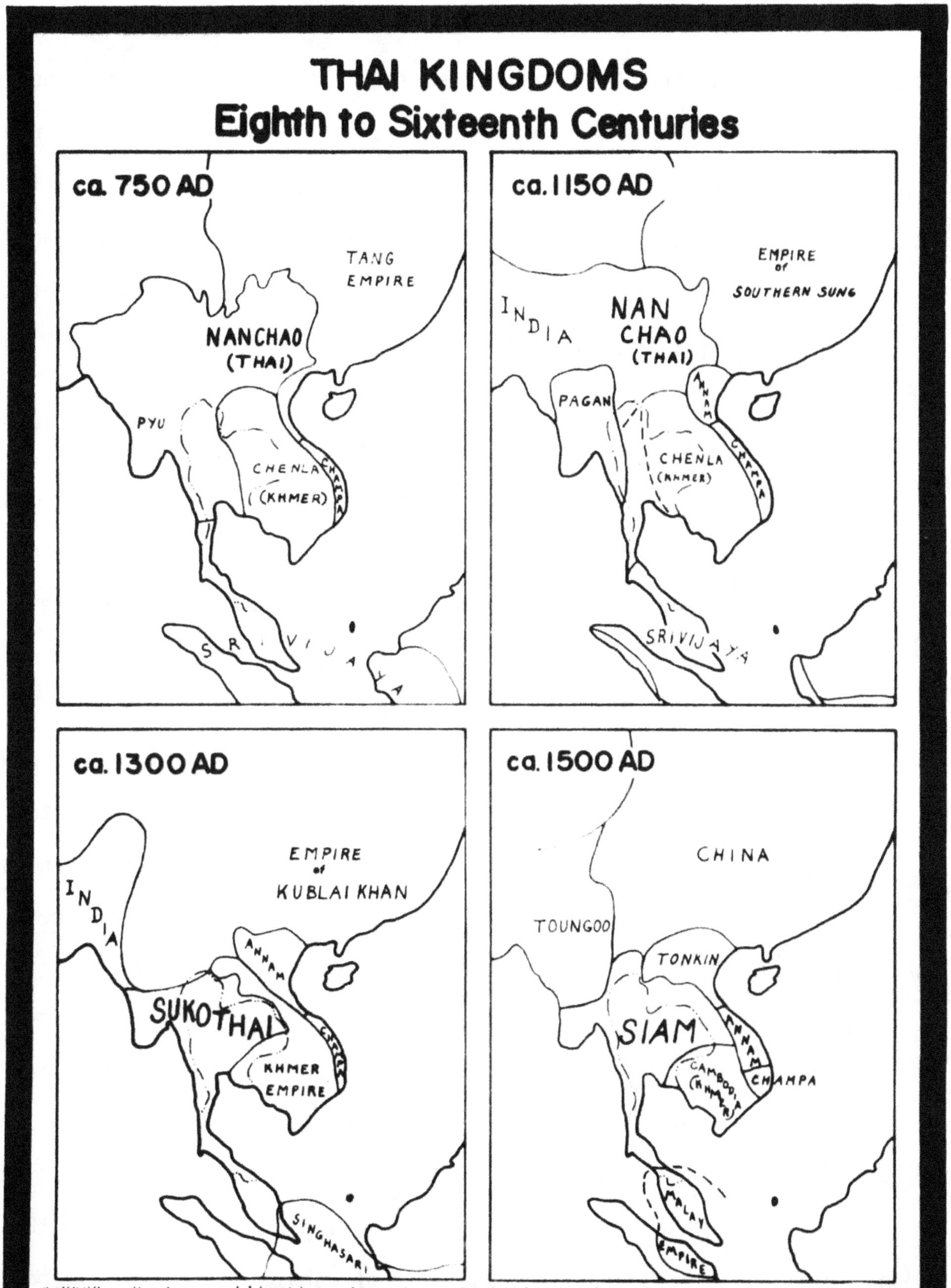

THAI KINGDOMS
Eighth to Sixteenth Centuries

ca. 750 AD — Tang Empire; Nanchao (Thai); Pyu; Chenla (Khmer); Champa; Srivijaya

ca. 1150 AD — India; Empire of Southern Sung; Nan Chao (Thai); Pagan; Annam; Chenla (Khmer); Champa; Srivijaya

ca. 1300 AD — India; Empire of Kublai Khan; Annam; Sukothai; Champa; Khmer Empire; Singhasari

ca. 1500 AD — China; Toungoo; Tonkin; Siam; Annam; Cambodia (Khmer); Champa; Malay Empire

SOURCE: Various publications listed in the bibliography

FIGURE 10

the South China Sea. As the Thai settled the river valleys, they displaced Mons and other earlier Southeast Asia settlers to higher, poorer, and less accessible lands. Where the Thai met strong resistance from one of the more advanced cultures they were stopped short of the lower river valleys and the sea, as they were in northwestern Vietnam by the Annamese people around the Gulf of Tonkin. Consequently, the main thrust of the Thai migration was funneled due south from Yunnan into present day Thailand and the Malay peninsula with periodic lateral spreading east into the Khmer and west into the Burman Kingdoms as weaknesses developed.[10]

(U) Since the 9th Century, the Thai have been in territorial disputes with neighbors on all sides. The Thai have at one time or another controlled the lands into Southern China on the north, to the lower reaches of the Irrawaddy River on the west, into Cambodia and the Annam Mountains on the east, and all of the Malay Peninsula on the south. The colonial period saw no complete control of Thailand by any European power; however, France took most of western Cambodia and Laos, and Britain took the easternmost Shan States of Burma and the northwestern and southernmost portions of the Malay Peninsula from Thailand. The demographic results are a Thai minority in each country of this area and several minority ethnic groups in Thailand.

(U) The Thai are the majority group in Thailand -- about 85 percent of the approximately 38,000,000 people. Chinese account for some 10 percent of the population, and Vietnamese, Indians, Malays, Cambodians, and tribal ethnic groups make up the remaining 5 percent. Among the Thai there is a reasonably strong sense of ethnic unity that extends across

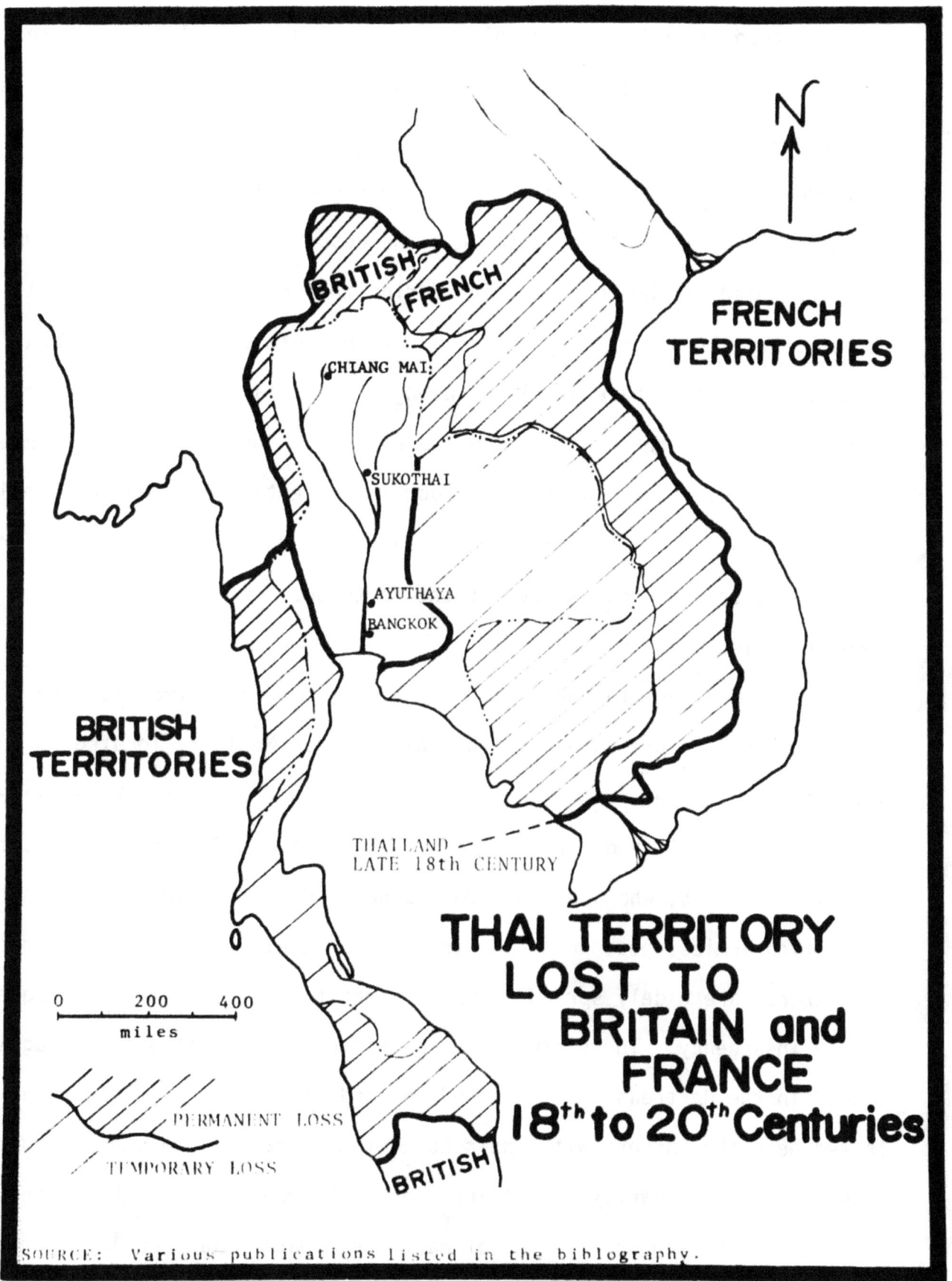

FIGURE 11

national borders and less strongly to some of the more closely related tribal groups (i.e., the Shans). Although it is this ethnic homogeneity that should be emphasized, there are four main groupings of Thai in Thailand -- the Northern Thai, the Northeastern Thai, the Southern Thai, and the Central Thai. The latter are the descendants of those Thai who migrated ahead of the Mongol armies during the second half of the 13th Century, and the others are primarily earlier settlers. Thus, several cultural variations have developed among ethnic Thai because of the relative isolation of their areas from one another. The Thai (mostly farmers and rural dwellers) are distributed across the entire country, with major concentrations in the central Chao Phraya River valley and the more fertile and better watered valleys of the North and Northeast as well as along the east coast of the South.

(U) In contrast to the Thai, the Chinese emigrated from eastern China and settled predominantly in urban areas. Most are located in and near Bangkok. Other concentrations are found in the central river valleys, the main valley of the Northeast, and in the Mid-South. The Kuomintang in the North, who are armed forces descendant from WWII and Chinese Revolution armies, pose no direct threat to the RTG. The Indians, small in numbers, are widely spread in urban areas, but are of little consequence to the insurgency. The Vietnamese are primarily restricted to "refugee zones" in the Northeast while Cambodians and Malays are mostly concentrated near the borders with their home ethnic areas. The other ethnic minorities are primarily hill tribesmen in the mountains of the northern provinces. The ethnic clusters of early Southeast Asian peoples are not

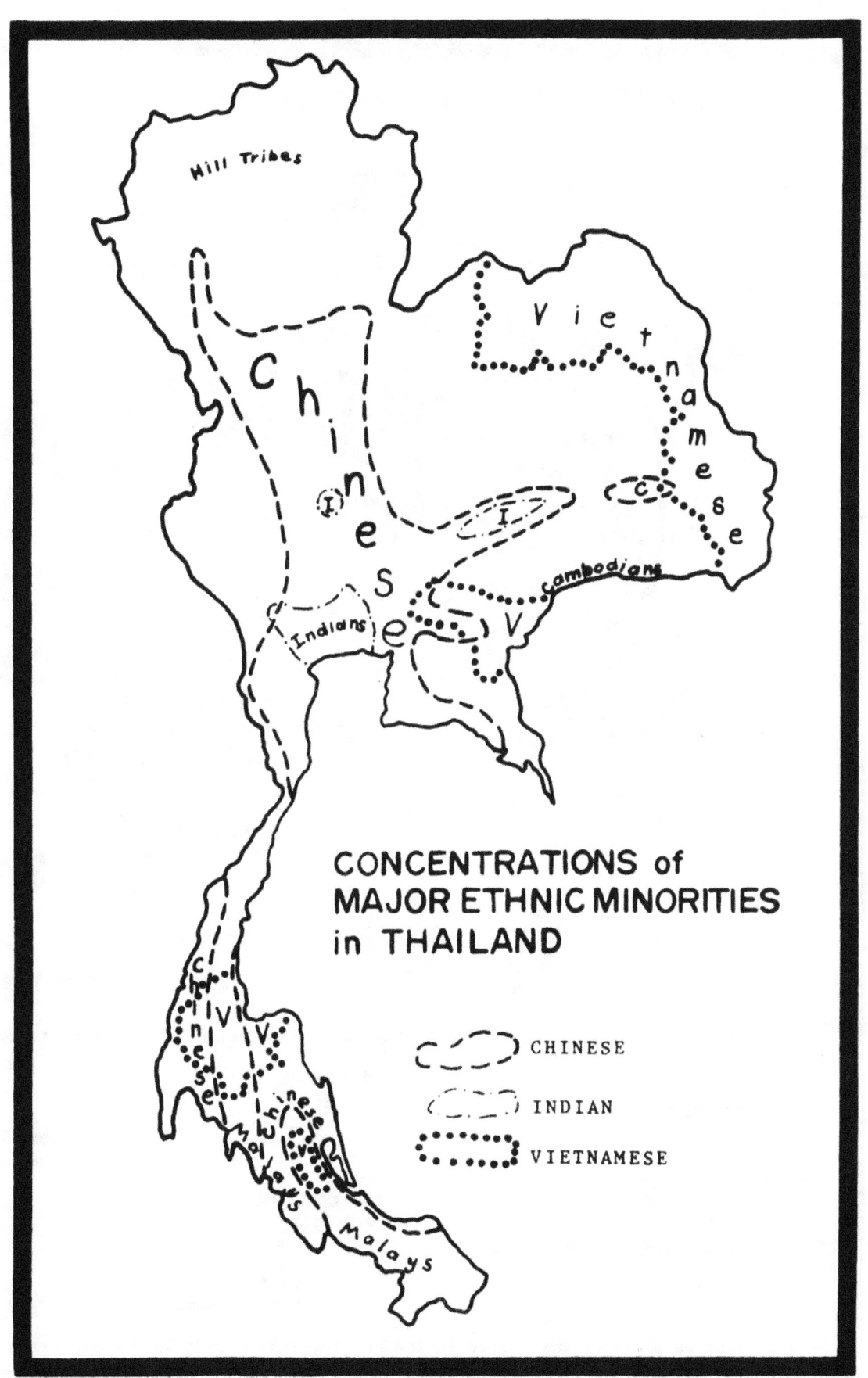

FIGURE 12

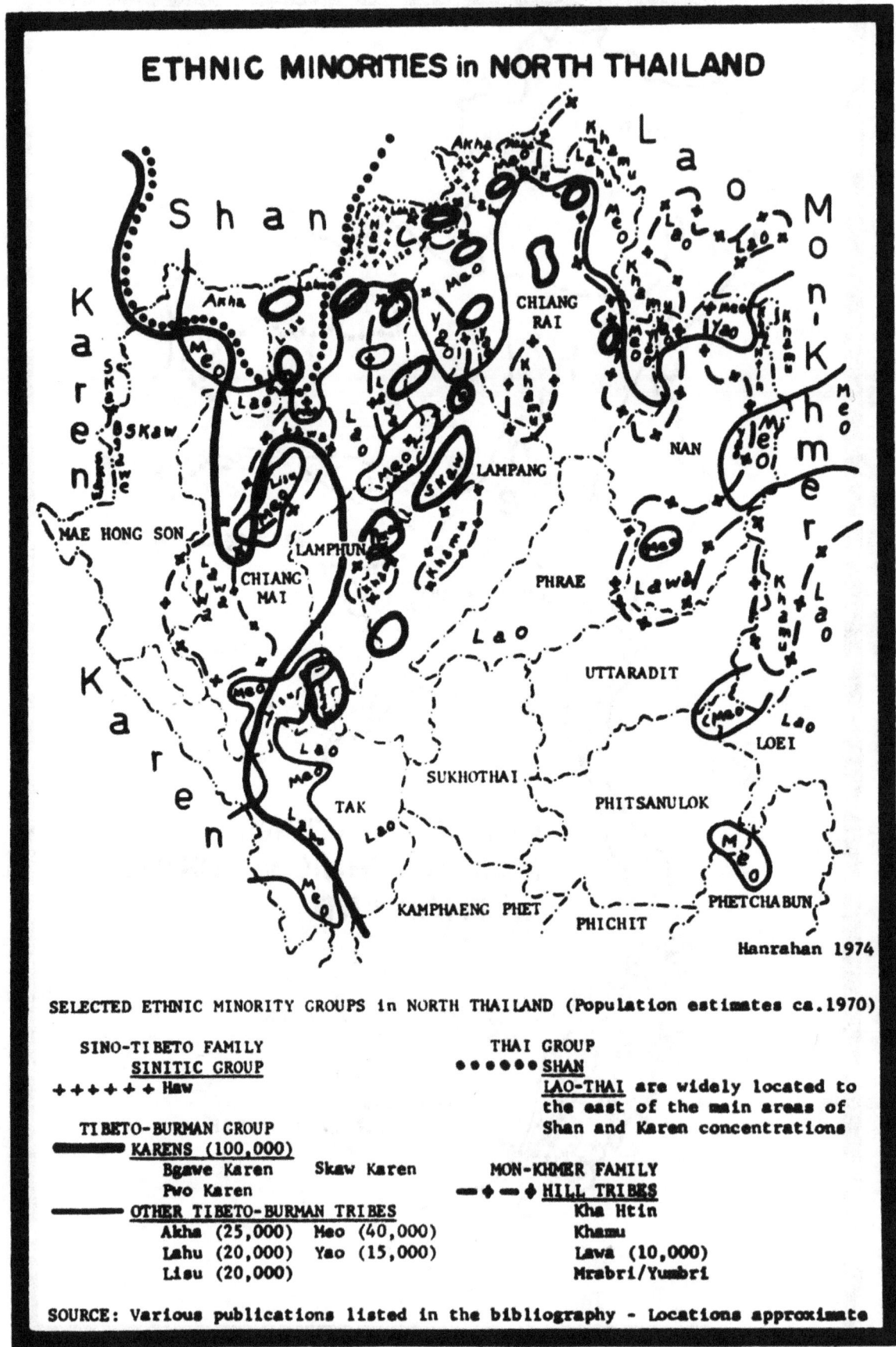

FIGURE 13

significant either in numbers or in insurgency potential. All of the border regions of Thailand contain some insurgent elements among peoples from neighboring countries.

(C) While the Chinese and the Vietnamese minorities provide CTs with funds and other support, large groups of Meo are actively waging war against the RTG and its forces. Military units of some Meo tribes, trained in Laos by the Pathet Lao, Chinese, and Vietnamese, have established strongholds in the mountains of Chang Rai and Nan and to a lesser degree in the highlands of other northern changwats. Meo units have attacked RTG forces and projects throughout most of the North including Tak and the tri-province area of Uttaradit, Phitsanulok, and Loei. Chinese, Sino-Thai, and some ethnic Thai have provided the political and military leadership.[11]

Cultural Institutions and the Complexities of Society in Thailand (U)

(U) The Meo and the Thai are both proud and would like to be left alone to pursue their own life forms, but in several other ways the Meo are the cultural antithesis of the Thai. The Thai are lowland Buddhists who have traditionally cultivated paddy rice and reserved the highlands for the King and government. It is into the game and forest preserves of the Thai King and ruling class that the mountain-dwelling animistic Meos have intruded. The Meo slash and burn valuable timber to clear fields in order to grow opium poppies and their subsistence food crops. They shift their crops to new fields every 2 to 3 years as the poor forest soils become depleted and do not reuse agriculture land for 25 years or longer. Consequently, as more and more Meo have migrated into Thailand from Laos during the past 10 years in order to avoid the fighting the Thai have seen vast areas of scarce timber reserves destroyed by these foreign interlopers whose traditional ways also break Thai drug and immigration laws.[12]

(C) Government programs to alleviate tensions have met with little success. The RTG attempts to resettle Meo to river bottom and other lowlands have antagonized the mountain-loving, individualistic Meo. Marketing difficulties associated with the crops that were substituted for the cash poppy crop have put some Meo near starvation. Resettlement plans and road building efforts have not been funded adequately. The result has been a growing conflict with the Meo as the RTG has tried to force the Meo to abide by Thai customs and laws.[13]

(U) The Thai are very conscious of ethnic ties, and discrimination against non-Thai has occurred often. The Chinese, Vietnamese, and Meo are widely distrusted, and even hated by some Thais. The Central Thai are richer than the Thai of the North, Northeast, and South, and generally consider themselves to be superior. This attitude of superiority is not lost on the Northern, Northeastern, and Southern Thai who in return view the Central Thai with a certain amount of suspicion and conflict-of-interest type distrust in relation to political activities.[14]

(U) The Northeastern Thai under Pridi Phanomyong tried to set up a Thai state with Laos across the Mekong. The politics of such irridentist actions are complex, but the cultural ties with the Lao majority, who are ethnically Thai, are unmistakable. As the Thai state grew with the capitals subsequently at Sukothai, Ayuthaya, and Bangkok during the 13th to 20th Centuries, overland communications with the Northeast improved very little until relatively recently. During this developmental period, ties were facilitated between Laos and the Northeast, and cultural similarities grew on both sides of the Mekong more easily than across the difficult terrain between the Chao Phrya River Basin and the Northeast. It was only with the French annexation of Laos less than 100 years ago that a national border began to hinder trans-Mekong movements of people who traditionally owed as much allegiance to the "Thai" King at Luang Prabang*[15] as they did to the Thai King at Bangkok.

(U) A comparable situation has existed in the South: the Malay-Thai are Muslim and look toward Malaya for direction in Islamic and certain other matters. The Buddhist and distant Thai government in Bangkok have been accused of a lack of understanding and concern for Malay heritage. Consequently movements to associate with Malaya have been numerous. CT activities have concentrated in the mid-South, but the bases of the CTO near the border have also contributed to political tension throughout the South. The North, however, has been more closely associated with the Central Region because of the better riverine communications. Thus, while some regional antagonisms have developed between Northern Thai and Central Thai, they are not significant in comparison to the difficulties between the RTG and Thai of the South and Northeast.

(U) Apart from regional differences among the Thai, there are significant variations and similarities characteristic of all of Thailand and Thai subcultures. The rural-urban dichotomy and the unequal distribution

---

* Laos

of wealth are increasing, and a lord-retainer relationship exists as a heritage of the absolute monarchy. There is a strong love of Buddha, King, and Country and intense suspicion of all historical enemies (i.e., Chinese, Vietnamese, Burmese, and Khmer). Yet Indian, Chinese, and anamistic ritualistic and stylistic forms color Thai life. The Thai offer a pleasant countenance which is a representation both of love of life and also of the stylistic, formalized structure of Thai life and society. Despite the formal structure of Thai society, however, room has remained for a degree of individual expression that is unique in South and East Asian cultures. Pleasure is an important goal in life. Duty is also important, whether it be to family, Buddha, or to an ideal, but there is more to life and trade offs are expected. Tolerance, apathy, and peacefulness are bywords of the Thai philosophy of life. The aversion to taking life, to violence, and to arguing permeate Thai society. The good accumulated in merit-making offsets any indiscretions, and shame (losing "face") is much more intolerable than sin. Consequently, the highly survivable Thai, who has adroitly bargained and maneuvered for centuries to preserve Thai unity and national independence by avoiding battles that he could not win, will fight violently when forced by circumstances in order to remove an unbearable shame.[16]

(U) The effect of Thai culture on the potential for insurgency in Thailand is somewhat contradictory. As one summation states, the situation is "Revolution In A Non-revolutionary Society."[17] Most of the Thai are not politically conscious: the peasant is still essentially a feudal vassal. The King and the RTG (since 1932) constitute the "feudal Lord." The peasant has been happy to receive protection, fair prices for crops, etc., in return for providing the lord with taxes, soldiers, etc. The Thai civil services in all capacities are extensions of the lord's power, and the interfaces with the elected village representatives are essentially decree-pronouncing sessions. In return for the direction of his political life by the RTG, the peasant has expected the RTG to assume the responsibility for those aspects of life beyond the individual's control -- the rains, market prices, etc. The traditional redress is through petitioning the King en masse, not by appealing to minor officials who have their personal status at stake. Representative government is a foreign cultural form and puts urban Thai in the position of representing predominantly rural Thailand. The system of 71 provinces (later 72) with district subdivisions replaced the King's regional chiefs in 1932 and has been generally choked with inefficient political appointees, mostly from the military at the gubernatorial and other high provincial levels. The number of military governors and the military dictatorship as the national form of government (several times since the overthrow of the absolute Monarchy) should not be viewed in the western sense. One US Foreign Service Officer stated, "These are politicians in uniform,"[18] more than conversely. The Royal Thai Army has emerged as the political power elite, and little change is likely to occur in spite of recent* invitations to politicians in uniform to leave military service. The result has been a system where status is reversed, conflict is avoided, loyalty is rewarded, and initiative is thwarted. The current challenges to the system come from student and

---

* After the October 1973 student demonstrations and change of government.

labor groups as well as from insurgents. The students are basically urban oriented, however, and while they offer some hope of gaining efficiencies in the political system, they do not as clearly promise effective change in the rural-urban inequities in standard of living, in economic well-being, or in political power.

(U) Some change in Thai society is inevitable, and the October 1973 student demonstrations that were instrumental in the ouster of Prime Minister Thanom Kittikachorn are indicative of the tensions that can develop. Potential tension-forming situations exist or are likely to occur in the political and economic structure as the population increases and becomes better educated. For example, the subsistence existence of the peasant in the Northeast was tolerable as long as nearly everyone farmed his own land. As the population increases and puts more stress on the land, both the number of landless farmers and the working force grow. The number of available jobs will increasingly lag behind the available workers unless some unforeseen change occurs. The potential consequences of large numbers of untenured farmers and unemployed workers are explosive, and the presence of the United States military as the largest employer in the Northeast further complicates the situation. The Thai power elite view the US military presence from good or a necessary evil, to a severe undermining of Thai customs and morality. There is no widespread dissatisfaction with the US bases among the Thai, especially not among businessmen and Thai employees, but the growing "political" energy of certain groups (i.e., the student and labor associations) could be directed at the United States at any time. In all areas of the country, wages and standards of living will increase for 10 years or more, but the Bangkok area will increase faster than elsewhere, and increasing numbers of people will be cut off from the general economic increase.[19]

(C) By concentrating in the preferred and higher status pursuits of government service and farming, the Thai have left the commercial endeavors to Chinese, and to a lesser degree to Indians. As in other Asian countries, these foreigners accumulate the wealth of the nation at the expense of the local nationals. In Thailand, a small number of Thai are leaders in commerce and are spread across the directorships of most of the larger, locally owned enterprises. In many cases, however, it appears that a working relationship has been set up between the Chinese (or other foreign) merchant and some local Thai government official. In effect, the Chinese have been allowed to operate, and part of their profits are "redistributed" to the local nationals. This practical arrangement may be indicative of the Thai ingenuity in finding a way to do what they want, but it also reflects the insufficient pay in the Thai civil service, the long-established method of acquiring one's personal fortune, and the unwillingness if not inability of law enforcement agencies to make more than token efforts to prevent graft. The potential of this system for creating political tensions and thwarting economic development is high.[20]

CHAPTER III

CAUSES OF INVOLVEMENT IN INSURGENCY (U)

(C) The Thai insurgency appears to be a direct result of the foreign policy of the CRP and the DRV.[21] To protect herself against the expansionist moves of China and North Vietnam, Thailand entered into security agreements with the United States. The more Thailand assisted the United States in the prosecution of the war in Vietnam and involved her security with the United States, the greater was the support to Thai insurgents from the CCP, the Lao Dong, the Lao communists, and even the Malayan communists. The support provided was primarily in the form of training and propaganda broadcast and leaflet equipment until the past few years when military equipment deliveries increased along with increased training.[22] The focus of this chapter is on group and individual susceptibility to insurgent overtures in Thailand.

Regional Discontent and Involvement Among Groups in Thailand (U)

(C) Certain minority groups have been susceptible to communist recruiting based on cultural conflicts. The Meo in the North would most likely prefer to be left alone and not to be put in the position of having to choose sides. However, being in cultural conflict with the Thai and harassed by RTG officials, the Meo have accepted military training and weapons from the communists. Political indoctrination and the communist "jungle soldier" life style of denial have not been equally well received. Attacks against the RTG support Meo feelings, but communistic ideals and philosophies are counter to Meo tradition. The Meo tolerated the first stages of communist recruiting involving friendly aid, but have been less than enthusiastic about the more advanced stages in some cases and have rebelled and defected.[23]

(C) Other hill tribes in the North, and Khmer and Malay-Thai groups in the East and South have also made the choice between what they considered the lesser of two evils and have become involved with communism. Cultural conflicts with the Thai have been emphasized in the recruiting efforts. Oppression by RTG officials, taxation, lack of police protection against bandits, and general discrimination have been main themes. Villages and communities remote from established RTG centers have been heavily indoctrinated and have often been taken over to serve as CT strongholds or supply and support points. As the CTs demonstrate that they are the major, strongest, or only force in an area, entire groups and often the whole area acknowledge the CTs as their patron or "lord." The CT have enhanced their survivability by establishing headquarters and other support centers in provincial and national boundary areas to take advantage of jurisdictional conflicts and the weaker governmental control at the far reaches of the political region.[24]

(C) The Chinese and Vietnamese seem to be more politically oriented toward communism. The Vietnamese minority in Thailand essentially are war refugees from WWII and from French-Viet Minh who fought in northern regions of Vietnam. Similarly, the Chinese in many cases are refugees from the warfare in China during this century. Both ethnic groups apparently have received communist cadre with new migrants, and indoctrination is probably based on individual more than group aspirations, discontents, and fears.[25]

(C) While the ultimate goal of the communist insurgency is to subvert the Thai society, there has been little direct threat against the entire Thai ethnic majority. Nevertheless, some targeting of the Phu-Thai in the Northeast has been underway, and in the future there will likely be increasing targeting of other essentially non-distinct subgroups of ethnic Thai. It is noteworthy that the insurgents are making any headway at all in the Thai culture whose traditions run so counter to the main tenets of communism.

Involving the Individual in Communist Insurgency (U)

(C) The various appeals of communist cadre stand or fall on their ability to reach the individual and through him the group. Throughout Thailand communist recruiting has been based upon practical aspects of daily life and very personal considerations, both in appeals and attacks. In addition, the recruiting is usually approached subtly with the view toward long-range gains rather than quick enrollment in the communist cause. To this end, handbooks for cadre provide doctrine in the form of general goals, but leave the specific tactics to the ingenuity of the recruiter. Tactical guidelines stress being friendly and becoming involved with targeted villagers. The types of tactics employed generally vary little across Thailand, and when they do, it is to take advantage of some local situation. Sharp and Rinkel, in their study, Revolution in a Non-revolutionary Society, The Process of Involvement in Rural Insurgency in Thailand,[26] analyze communist recruiting techniques in Thailand in some detail. This section is a paraphrased summary of their findings.

(C) The relationship between the insurgent and the Thai villager is subtle and complex, varying from a friendly peer association to armed dominance. Infinite exploitation varieties occur within the extremes of possible relationships, but the insurgent psychological operations may be considered as occurring in several steps, each having different objectives. The "commitment development steps" are: (1) choosing a target village; (2) making initial contact or penetrating the village; (3) developing relationships with the villager and establishing influence positions; (4) overtly propagandizing; (5) gaining commitments from the villager to join the insurgents or to provide them support; and (6) consolidating the insurgent control. In each step, four general groupings of psychological approach alternatives may be applied: (1) efforts to create, develop, and exploit the individual's incentives or aspirations; (2) attempts to create, develop, and exploit the individual's grievances; (3) efforts to establish a position of power, status, or authority; and (4) efforts to establish empathetic or legitimate peer relationships. Using this framework, Sharp and Rinkel outline the typical sets of alternative approaches that are employed in the steps of (1) initial contacts, (2) developing relationships, (3) persuasive propaganda, and (4) establishing commitment.

(C) <u>Initial Contacts</u> seldom call for any political action because of the apolitical nature of Thai village life. Villagers normally expect little from the government, and therefore ready-made political issues for insurgent exploitation only occur rarely as in the case of long-standing conflict of the Meo with the RTG. One often-used method of contact is through relationship ties (ties with the immediate family, in some cases, and with the extended family or clan in others). Because the Thai family is not a tightly knit unit, these relationship contacts must be augmented by other ties to survive when confronted with conflict. The individualism of Thai society also makes friendship and acquaintance ties very fragile in the face of any adversity, but the insurgent can acquire information about other villagers from his friends and acquaintances and gain a certain degree of general acceptance from regularly being seen in their company.

(C) In the absence of exploitable kinship or friendship ties, the insurgent recruiter adopts an accepted social role as a cover for his activities. The villagers view merchants, spirit doctors, monks, and similar people as representing little threat. When the insurgent can not only assume one of these low threat roles, but also establish the status of education, wealth, wide travel, and other esteemed situations, he can achieve deferential and positive acceptance instead of mere tolerance. If the insurgent can successfully project power and authority to the villagers, more rapid and lasting acceptance develops. Since Thai culture respects a position of achievement and disdains unpleasantness, little direct opposition can be generated against apparent power and authority.

(C) Developing Relationships is probably the most important step of the commitment developing process. The villager's fragile acceptance of the initial insurgent contact is strengthened by model behavior by the insurgent recruiter over long periods of time. The recruiter avoids overt argumentation and programmatic appeals unless he has a secure status position and concentrates instead on conforming to behavioral norms even more scrupulously than other villagers. He enhances his status by demonstrating his composure and knowledge in the village informal discussions and also in providing civic action assistance. Helping develops certain obligations on the part of those helped, and the insurgent is able to accumulate "credits" to be used later. The insurgent working within the social fabric of the village also associates the villager with communists and insurgent-sponsored projects, thereby opening the possibility of threats of exposure to RTG officials should the villager be hesitant in providing favors to the insurgents in the future. Intimidation, threat, and force are all acceptable and effective tools. There is, however, little evidence of terror being employed as a basic approach in developing villager relationships, and assassinations are used defensively against government agents, police, village defense corps, school teachers, and other RTG officials as well as against insurgent defectors. This is the step in which personal ties to the insurgent recruiter are expanded and cemented.

(C) Persuasive Propaganda is the critical and sensitive phase of institutionalizing personal ties. The insurgent tries to transform his personal acceptance by the peasants into an acceptance of the insurgent organization and movement. At this point the appeals are still emotional rather than rational. The behavioral characteristics of the villager and his village are used to politicize the insurgent's power, authority, and status relationships. The insurgent exploits villager grievances and aspirations while emphasizing the disruptiveness of RTG efforts in the countryside. In the classless village society, the insurgent characterizes himself as another one of the farmers, all of whom are being exploited by the corrupt urban changers of traditional Thai life. Under the communists, the traditional life will be made better but not changed. In contrast, the insurgent argues, whenever the RTG approaches the village, it is to interfere with and disrupt the traditional Thai way of life. When the RTG trains local officials, it is really training agents to spy on the village; RTG security forces are deployed for suppression of the farmer; taxes are extortion. Thus, the insurgents are the traditionalists and the RTG officials are the revolutionaries. The insurgents are the protectors of Thai rural virtues against external threats by the urban ruling clique. The insurgents maneuver the villagers into a political hierarchy using the Thai peasant's tradition of deference to authority, his aversion to competitive behavior in his immediate group, his willingness to accept whatever everyone else has accepted, and his responsiveness to personal and individualistic treatment at each stage of the recruiting process. In short, the insurgent movement legitimizes itself in traditional terms understood by the villager and at the expense of the remote, urban society with its unfamiliar and mysterious ways.

(C) <u>Establishing Commitment</u> is getting the villager to join the movement or to provide it with some positive support. Capitalizing on felt obligations, eliminating alternatives perceived by the villager, playing on villager deference to his authority, and offering the villager personal gain, the insurgent recruiter entices a commitment from his target. The obligation for help with the farm, for instance, gets a favor from the villager for some support for the insurgent cause. The support involves the villager, so threat of exposure to the RTG might elicit an introduction of the insurgent recruiter to a relative. The relative joins, so the original villager is now obligated for his relative's safety while his relative is associated with the insurgent movement. Thus, felt obligation may expand and, in conjunction with low level threat from an authority figure, limit the villager's perception of what he can do to only one choice -- remaining in the insurgent movement.

(C) While the villager's passivity, exploited through "bandwagon" appeals, feelings of obligation, and threats to his serene rural life, has been instrumental in obtaining and prolonging commitment, purely personal offers and incentives are a major part of the insurgent recruiting. Individualism and other Thai-Buddhist cultural traits have created a situation where there is potential status in and little constraint to seizing opportunities when presented by the insurgent recruiter as he encourages the villager's desire for personal advancement or adventure. The effort of gaining a commitment from a villager appears to become in large part one of selecting the proper combination of personal offers that will be most effective on him. The insurgent has a long list to choose from -- one that includes money, rank, weapons, adventure, travel, education, farming assistance, and easy work.

(C) Whether or not the insurgent recruiter succeeds, Sharp and Rinkel point out, depends greatly on the personal idiosyncracies of the insurgent agents, the target villagers, and the RTG representatives at hand. Analysis attempting to isolate psychological or background factors that would indicate susceptibilities to insurgent recruitment showed there were no clear overall correlations. Factors like occupation, wealth, age, sex, and education were important in individual cases, but they varied in non-regular ways as did the methods of the insurgents in time and place to support changing insurgent objectives in a variety of situations. The consequences for the insurgency appear to be continual trouble with Thai individualism, and the consequences for the RTG's counterinsurgency program seem to be the necessity for an effective intelligence function and a practical, flexible approach to rural development and change.

PART B -- COUNTERINSURGENCY: EVOLVING RTG AND US EFFORTS

STATEMENT OF AMBASSADOR LEONARD UNGER (5 March 1973)

(TAB J TO THE <u>GENERAL CONCEPT FOR US SUPPORT OF THAI COUNTERINSURGENCY</u>)

TO: Members of the Mission
    Executive Council

FROM: The Ambassador

SUBJECT: Supplemental Guidance on RTG Counterinsurgency Programs

1. As you are aware, we have recently been informed that the Thai have modified somewhat their tactical approach toward meeting the Communist insurgency, although the Government's basic strategy is unchanged.

2. On the military side, it appears that the Thai have decided, for the present at least, that large scale frontal assaults on base areas of concentrated insurgent strength, along the lines of Operation Phu Kwang in 1972, are inadvisable for a variety of reasons. During the campaign this year, including JTX-16, RTA has stressed operations against TPLAF supply lines and support facilities and has stepped up small-scale penetration actions into areas of CT strength. The current campaign has been successful in achieving these limited objectives. This has probably reinforced the Thai view that more sustained pressure against the Communists is preferable under present circumstances to cyclical, massive assault on base areas. Coupled with this is the position that increased emphasis needs to be given to improving the quality and effectiveness of government as a means of winning or retaining the support of the villagers.

3. As projected in the National CI Program and revealed in discussions with Thai leaders, this approach has four major elements:

    a. <u>Systematic Improvement and Strengthening of Government</u> in the areas which surround the insurgent main base areas. This would include village self-defense and social and economic improvement programs; strengthened police and militia forces patrolling in the vicinity of villages; police investigations of subversive elements; the amnesty program; and integration of these measures under augmented district offices (OCC).

    b. <u>Police and militia actions</u> to control population and supply movements and interdict access routes into or out of CT base areas.

    c. <u>Sustained but selective penetration</u> into CT base areas by small military units to harass and tie down the insurgent main forces, disrupt their supply lines, interrupt their contacts with CT controlled villages, gather intelligence, and, in general, turn the Communists' own tactics back against them. For these purposes the RTA leadership plans to make greater efforts to use smaller units (platoons and squads). The RTA is also in the process of forming small Ranger/Volunteer units for this purpose.

    d. <u>In the North, assistance to hill populations</u> by improving re-settlement centers, upland agriculture and crop substitution, organizing and arming hilltribe volunteer defense units, and adopting a "civic action," labor-intensive approach to strategic road construction and other security-police developments.

4. These measures are aimed at gradually cutting off the insurgents from the Thai population near CT base areas and at creating subsequent opportunities to engage the insurgent main forces with regular RTA units under more favorable conditions. We also encourage continued development for CI of RTA units manned with conscripts; when adequately trained and led such units can defeat the RPLAF.

5. This memorandum will serve to incorporate the concepts outlined above into our Mission Guidelines and thus to supplement the <u>Mission Concept for Support of Thai Counterinsurgency</u>. Please circulate it to your personnel.[27]

Embassy of the United States of America
Bangkok

CHAPTER IV

THE ROYAL THAI GOVERNMENT'S EFFORTS TO MEET THE THREAT (U)

(S) The Thai government has been aware of communists in Thailand since the 1920s and has been reacting to their presence ever since. Rewards for arrests of communists, police raids, and deportations were the early responses to agents entering Thailand from China and elsewhere in Southeast Asia. The National Assembly passed legislation making communist organizations illegal in 1933. The Act concerning communism supplemented existing criminal codes prohibiting subversion and revolutionary activity. In 1946, the RTG repealed the 1933 anticommunist act in order to preclude a Soviet veto of Thailand's bid for United Nations membership, but in 1952 enacted another strict anticommunist law in response to the victory in China and the heightened potential for subversion in Thailand. Initially, control measures were primarily directed at the Chinese, as much because they were cornering too much wealth as because they represented the bulk of the communists. Controls were also placed on the Vietnamese refugees in Thailand because of concern over Viet Minh intentions after their forces invaded Laos in 1953. The Vietnamese who had fled to Thailand to avoid WWII and subsequent fighting were sympathetic to Vietnamese nationalism and the Viet Minh, although the majority of the refugees were not communists. Viet Minh recruiters were active among the Vietnamese in Thailand, however, and were a source of concern to the RTG. Specific RTG suppression actions were intricately entangled with the complexities of Thai politics, and police roundups and detention continued to be the primary counterinsurgency tactics through the 1950s and into the 1960s.[28]

(S) Through the 1950s and into the 1960s it appeared to RTG officials that communist insurgents were just one of the many minor subversive elements in the countryside. The RTG was strongly coup and power-balance conscious, as it remains to a large degree today. The widespread incidents of banditry, cattle rustling, killings, and other lawlessness were viewed as unconnected crimes of local concern, and handled in that manner by the RTG until after the 1957 coup of General Sarit Thanarat, Commander-in-Chief of the Royal Thai Army (RTA). General Sarit and his followers, including Generals Thanom Kittikachorn and Charasuthien, commanded wide popular support and were able to act more decisively than previous administrations. Martial law was declared, and a new Interim Constitution virtually gave the Prime Minister carte blanche in suppressing subversion. Whether or not he was playing on US politics and taking a proven avenue to US aid is open to speculation. Whatever his motivation, General Sarit did take CI action at the national level: he established the National Security Command Center (NSCC) and Mobile Development Units (MDUs) in the face of general RTG feeling that a communist insurgency was impossible in the countryside dedicated to King and Buddha as well as steeped in Thai tradition so basically contrary to the teaching of communism. The armed attacks in the Northeast during 1965 subdued the "impossible insurgency" argument. By December 1965 the formation of the Communist Suppression Operations Center (CSOC) was announced, and the RTG had the second national "overall coordinating" center operating approximately a year later. Increasingly, the official position of the RTG into the 1970s is that the communist insurgency is a threat. That is also the opinion of many Thai officials assigned to CI policy making, but the majority of Thai probably still subscribe to the impossible insurgency view and feel that a serious communist threat is mostly in the minds of foreigners.[29]

RTG CI Strategy and Approaches (U)

(S) The main principle underlying RTG counterinsurgency policies and programs is that the unrest which leads to insurgency grows out of economic need and frustration of expectations. Improving the conditions of life in insurgent areas will cure the subversion. Consequently, RTG strategy focuses on creating an immunity to communist appeals and developing popular attachments to the RTG. Rural developmental, informational, and psychological programs support these purposes. In addition, the RTG strategy calls for direct suppression of CT activities through programs of improving village security, developing intelligence agents and networks, and military/police operations against insurgent units. The central theme is reaching the rural population -- influencing the villagers by exemplary behavior and avoiding any actions that might alienate them.*[30]

(S) From a theoretical viewpoint, RTG planning to carry out its strategic objectives has been essentially sound, innovating, and enlightened; in practice, however, it is somewhat belated, structured to protect the political power balance, and employs a defensive "containment" approach. Thai values drive the social and other systems in Thailand and status and money are ultimate values. Therefore, the need to protect the existing power balance (status) has been a reality of life and has resulted

---
* (S) Contrary to the central theme, however, there have been numerous instances where the behavior and actions of counterinsurgency forces and RTG officials have alienated the villagers.

in the RTA, the Royal Thai Air Force (RTAF), the National Police, the Border Patrol Police (BPP), the Provincial Police (PP), and other RTG agencies each receiving a share of the CI effort and its funding. General Sarit had the power to see that the NSCC assumed the full spectrum of its designed responsibilities. However, after General Sarit's death (which occurred before NSCC, under the operational control of Air Marshal Dawee Chulasap, could barely start a few improvement measures) Sarit's power in the RTG was divided between Thanom and Praphat. Praphat headed one power group evidenced by his titles of Commander-in-Chief of the RTA, Minister of the Interior, and Deputy Prime Minister. The Ministry of the Interior (MOI) is the parent organization of important CI activities including the police and the Department of Local Administration (DOLA) under which the Provincial Governments operate. Thanom as Prime Minister administered RTG efforts in foreign and economic matters and controlled the armed services other than the RTA. With Air Marshal Dawee (a close friend of Sarit and Thanom) heading NSCC, Praphat saw to it that NSCC CI responsibilities and funding were eroded in favor of CSOC which he commanded. CSOC was essentially under the operational direction of RTA General Saiyund Kerdhpol, the Chief of the CSOC Operational Directorate, a man who also has been an innovator and a spokesman for a "modern thinking" group in the RTA. CSOC activities began to expand and increasingly more RTA assets were requested for field deployment under CSOC operational control prompting the RTA to take over CSOC field apparatus in 1967 in order to protect RTA status. The RTA attack on CSOC resulted largely from personal dissatisfactions with Dawee and from jeopardized vested interests.[31]

(C) The CSOC concept was to coordinate the CI efforts of civilian, police, and military under a single managing and planning agency, which translated into CSOC acquiring the following general areas of responsibility:

- Management of joint suppression forces in the field
- Coordinating actions to counter communism in Thailand and abroad
- Suppression of communist insurgents
- Coordination of RTG agencies' efforts in preventing and suppressing communist operations
- Conducting psychological operations (PSYOPS) aimed at the people and the insurgents.

(C) Unfortunately, in practice CSOC was never given the authority or power needed to meet those responsibilities. The actual structure and operation of CSOC has been evolving since its inception.* The specific paths of this evolution, and the various RTG agencies formed (and their employment), are detailed in the reports of several US agencies. Among these reports are the Research Analysis Corporation (RAC) Histories, prepared under the direction of Roswell B. Wing, and Douglas S. Blaufarb's Rand report on Thai Counterinsurgency, both prepared for Advanced Research Projects Agency (ARPA).[32] The following overview of the RTG CI forms and implementing agencies is paraphrased from these two sources.

(U) In the attempt to improve the rural environment, the MDUs were the first Thai effort. They were limited in their conception and worked almost entirely in the Northeast. The teams were military with some civilian technicians and operated one to a district consisting of some 12

---

* (U) Presently, operations are through Communist Suppression Operations Regions (CSORS) (see Figure p. 4).

53

villages. By 1964, a broader approach was developed under the Accelerated Rural Development program (ARD). Starting as a program to build rural roads with local planning and resources, it expanded to provide funding and operational authority to province governors for local developmental projects. It included support to farmers' cooperatives, farm youth groups, and other local programs requiring funds and technical assistance. ARD was put under the Prime Minister's direct control in 1966 after political problems and bureaucratic rivalries in DOLA threatened its viability. Other RTG Ministries sponsored various programs to improve rural government below the provincial level. The Developing Democracy program concerned itself with training Tambon* councils to deal with local problems and provided funds for small self-help projects. MOI's Community Development program gave village leaders training in dealing with developmental problems and also provided funds. The Ministry of Health had its regular public health programs and also established special Mobile Medical Teams to operate in insurgent areas, as well as Protein Food Development, Potable Water, and Rural Health programs. The Ministries of Agriculture and Education set up an agribusiness program and trade-skills education programs, respectively, in the villages. DOLA's District Officer Academy was also a training attempt to extend effective government to the people. In addition to these mostly parochial efforts of established Ministries, the RTG formed and directed more long-range and national scale developmental programs such as roadbuilding, airport development, training, and agricultural extension and education. Many of these Thai national- and regional-scale

---

* (U) See glossary of terms.

programs have been supported by the Southeast Asia Treaty Organization (SEATO), the Colombo Plan, the United Nations, and directly by some two dozen nations.[33]

(C) Between the longer-range, more purely environmental development programs described immediately above and the direct suppression activities sketched below are the localized civic action programs of Thai military and paramilitary forces. The purpose of civic actions is to gain the acceptance of the people around the camps and in the patrol areas of RTG armed forces. The anticipated immediate benefit to the RTG forces is intelligence about subversive and insurgent activity. The RTA began creating Special Operations Center (SOC) posts along the Thai borders in 1963. The 84 men in each of the eight posts included intelligence and PSYOPS specialists as well as soldiers trained in medical care and basic civic actions skills. In patrolling some 75 kilometers out from their posts, the men performed needed services for the villages. The Remote Area Security Development (RASD) program began in 1960. Under the direction of the BPP, the program focused on key villages in provinces with large tribal populations. Most of the villages have been in Nan, Chiengrai, Petchabun, and Phitsanuloke; and Meo, Yao, Lisu, and Lahu tribal groups have been involved. Select policemen of the BPP received training in medical and agricultural aid, and some men from each key village were trained in civic actions. Together with trained tribesmen, the BPP built STOL* airstrips, animal pens, schools, dispensaries, and provided education, agricultural advice, and medical aid. In other areas where there was less concentration,

---

* (U) Short takeoff and landing.

BPP units built Development Centers to demonstrate developmental projects, established schools with police constables as teachers, and dispensed medical aid while on patrol through the countryside. The civic actions programs have all been reasonably effective as far as they have gone in persuance of their limited objective of gaining local intelligence useful in insurgency prevention and suppression.[34]

(C) The suppression activities of the RTG aimed at seeking out and eliminating insurgent armed forces are conducted by an assortment of Thai police, military, and paramilitary forces and programs. The RTA has been a major element in CI efforts because of its political power and the size of national forces under its control. It has contributed the SOCs, Special Forces, and infantry to CI operations. Hunter-capture teams and Long-Range Reconnaissance and Patrol (LRRP) teams have been under development to give the RTA CI capability beyond major sweeps by conventional line units. RTA, police, and RTAF air units support CI operations when called upon, through coordination at the Direct Air Support Center (DASC) located in each regional headquarters. The BPP, by virtue of their mission and the lack of roads along the borders, have had some patrol aircraft since the 1950s, and the Thai National Police Department since 1968-1969. An integral command and control of RTG aircraft including support to the CI commands was effected through the Tactical Air Control System (TACS). The main units of the BPP, however, are line platoons which have been deployed to the 25 kilometer border zone that they patrol from their base camps. In addition to the line platoons and developmental platoons, the BPP developed Mobile Reserve Platoons (MRPs) and Special Weapons Platoons for reaction forces to suppress insurgent bands. These forces and the Special Action Forces (SAF) of the PP were the main CI suppression forces during the period 1965-1967 before the RTA took control of CI suppression. Since RTA control, RTA units have been largely employed as CI reaction forces instead of similarly organized police units, and the police units have been allowed to erode. Other paramilitary forces used by the RTG for CI suppression are the Kuomintang and tribal auxiliaries. The Border Security Volunteer Teams (BSVTs) are controlled by BPP cadre and the RTA sponsors the Hill-Tribe Volunteers (RTVs). Developing and using these two forces has not been enthusiastically and continuously supported by the RTG which has also somewhat been the case with the Volunteer Defense Corps (VDC), an organization used both as a CI strike force and for local security.[35]

(C) Local security is the function of various police and militia-like organizations including the VDC. The VDC was established during the early 1950s and has had erratic support since then because of its military type structure and association with the police. VDC status has been carefully limited; it is managed by DOLA, the RTA handles recruiting and training, and deployed units are usually commanded by the police of RTA. The organizational command of VDC units rests with the province governor, and VDC companies have been assigned to provinces, platoons to districts, and squads to villages with combinations of village squads and district platoons forming district companies as well. Several schemes have appeared over the years of village security, but Thai politics have precluded the more ambitious, nation-wide security groups. The various mostly-local remnants of early pilot programs include Village Security Development Units (VSDUs) under DOLA, Muban Police under the PP that operated out of Tambon police stations, Joint Security Teams (JSTs) of VDCs led by provincial policemen or army noncommissioned officers (NCOs), and Volunteer Protection Teams (VPTs) organized by the governor of Ubon and trained by RTA Special Forces. Other village protection organizations exist and still more have been in existence. In addition, one must note that there are Metropolitan Police, Railway Police, Marine Police, Highway Patrol Police, Immigration Police, and the Special Branch (SB) for counterespionage and security as well as the BPP and the PP. An early CI realization was the need to revitalize the police in order to provide reasonable rural security. The PP became the focus of CI training, as well as for facility and equipment upgrading. The village radio project implemented by the TNPD (installation and maintenance) and under DOLA (for operational control) has provided much needed rural communications, and other technical aspects of police operations have been improved.[36]

(S) Intelligence-gathering, informational, and PSYOPS programs have received considerable attention from the RTG in support of the full range of governmental responsibilities from national strategy to the day-to-day workings of the military, police, and civilian agencies. Many Thai in government understand the need for accurate intelligence to specifically target insurgents and their activities so that the population at large is not turned away from an uninformed RTG reduced to inaction or to striking blindly at entire population groups. The RTG operates a variety of intelligence organizations, some of which are more directly aimed at CI. The SB, a part of the Criminal Investigation Division of the TNPD, collects data on subversive groups and activities, conducts clearances on government employees, guards dignitaries, and oversees censorship. The BPP, the PP, and the Armed Forces through the joint Armed Forces Security Center (AFSC) and the RTA's LRRPT and Hunter-Capture Teams, as well as other RTG agencies, gather intelligence on affairs ranging from counterintelligence to counterinsurgency and political reliability. Efforts to centralize CI intelligence collection produced the Joint Security Centers (JSCs) in provinces with high insurgency threat and created an intense focus on intelligence in CSOC. CSOC and other Thai organizations employed PSYOPS and informational operations in support of CI, but while these topics received considerable attention from the Thai, direction and execution often relied on US initiative due to reasons of politics and status -- problems that permeate the entire RTG CI effort. Furthermore, although the RTG created a large, relatively centralized counterinsurgency intelligence apparatus, principal intelligence organizations in most insurgent areas have neglected collecting and analyzing information about insurgency at the local level. Intelligence available to local officials is generally limited and dated.[37]

Problems and Trends in RTG CI Efforts (U)

(C) Problems encountered in Thai CI efforts center around a small number of institutions and situations -- some typical of I/CI in developing countries, some uniquely Thai. The rural-urban dichotomy coupled with problems of intelligence gathering, analysis, and dissemination resulted in general lack of perception in the RTG and the Thai intelligencia of the communist insurgent threat until after armed attacks began in 1965.

The difficulties in allocating scarce resources to suppression versus development, or to one region versus another, have also been compounded by incomplete intelligence and faulty assumptions. Institutional forms in government and traditions in Thai culture and religion contribute to delaying perception of the insurgent threat and to diluting the effectiveness of execution of CI planning. Training government employees to be effective suffers from all of these problems and so, consequently, does getting information to villagers about RTG development and security efforts. Because, short of revolution, traditions and institutions can change only slowly, the RTG has put high emphasis on training and intelligence and has been trying to increase effectiveness in CI with pilot programs and new institutions. The overall trend in RTG CI is for sustained emphasis on intelligence gathering, research, training, and planning based on the best information available, while, as best the RTG can by trial and error, getting around institutional and situational constraints of the kind described elsewhere -- all the while keeping the people in mind and disrupting their life as little as possible.[38]

(C) Lack of information has been probably the most serious difficulty for effective CI. Seemingly isolated banditry and other crimes had been concerted CT activity for years before any general realization of that fact in Bangkok. The completely different orientation of life in the sophisticated primate city enhanced a complacency about all being well in the traditional, religious countryside. Occasional trips by officials from Bangkok or the provincial capitals got little real information from peasants suspicious of the "tax collectors" who have seldom returned anything to the village and who have always hurried back to the city. The insurgent recruiters have used such a variety of approaches that each village also has to be "infiltrated" by the government in order to gather information about how to counter the insurgents' approach and destroy their infrastructure. For instance, so little was known about the various hill tribes that early RTG efforts were largely counterproductive. The Hill Tribe Institute and such agencies as the Military Research and Development Center (MRDC) hopefully will sustain the trend to greater RTG knowledge and awareness. Other efforts and programs to gather village information and to show a RTG presence and to provide security point up another difficulty for effective CI.[39]

(S) That village security forces operated under six different auspices shows the program proliferation resulting from the status balancing in the RTG. Something of CI for everyone was carried out to the extent that four different road building organizations, three different medical programs, three air forces, and two different police reaction forces, as well as the RTA, have been involved in CI. Funding going down the chains of command of the armed forces, the police, and the numerous government ministries has dissipated the thrust of CI as well as created a complex nightmare of the command and control. The status balancing has contributed to inappropriate tactics as shown by the ineffective RTA sweeps by line units and the counterproductive bombing and burning of hill tribe villages. Had the power groups had forewarning of what roles CI would require, they might have created the proper tactics and forces within their own organization, an undertaking requiring effective intelligence. The tradition of protecting one's status at the expense of performance, in turn, supports keeping one's intelligence data instead of pooling it for national benefit. Prisoner interrogation, the rallier program, agricultural improvement, and most other reasonably conceived approaches have been hindered if not dissipated by similar status or individualis-caused problems of coordination in the field, at the provincial level, and in Bangkok.[40]

(C) What the Thai need is a CI plan that is national in scale, long-range, country-wide in application, and very comprehensive in its integration of developmental, security, and suppression aspects. However, the plan must be flexible enough to change with the times and local conditions. It has to employ a mix of CI approaches and tactics to keep constant pressure on the insurgents on all fronts. It must effectively employ the approximately 10 percent of the Thai budget allocated to CI through 1973 and be ready to expand as necessary. Most important, it must be a plan that operates to satisfy the needs of the people using a people to people, personal, face to face basis in rural areas. The RTG has a well conceived approach to CI along these lines and is slowly pursuing such a plan with US and other help.*[41] Hopefully in the future, performance will begin to match the planning in quality.

---

*(U) However, the RTG has not yet gotten very far with implementing such a plan at village level.

CHAPTER V

THE ROLE OF THE UNITED STATES IN THAI COUNTERINSURGENCY (U)

(C) US CI assistance to Thailand has been multifaceted and dates from the early 1950s, a time of Chinese Communist conquest of mainland China, the Korean War, and an expanding communist threat to Southeast Asia. Aid funds earmarked for China were diverted to other Asian countries, and developmental aid to Thailand began with projects like the dredging of Bangkok harbor.[42] Indirect US aid to Thai CI through development assistance of many kinds and more direct equipment and training aid to the various Thai CI organizations accelerated during the 1960s. In the early 1970s US aid had begun to wane with general reductions in foreign aid by Congress. The United States has been one of some two dozen nations providing developmental and CI aid to Thailand under the auspices of the United Nations, regional treaties,* and bilateral agreements. As in the case of RTG CI efforts, the portion of US aid applicable to CI is impossible to distinguish separately from general developmental aid due to the indirect effect of development on CI, and to some degree, it is also difficult to determine exactly where developmental/CI efforts are purely those of the Thai or purely those of the US Mission. US contributions to Thai CI have been on the order of one half as much as the Thai have budgeted themselves for CI -- some 8 to 10 percent of their annual budget.[43]

(C) US involvement in Southeast Asia increased rapidly during the 1960s and so did US objectives concerning Thailand. The United States

---
* (S) One such treaty was the Southeast Asia Treaty Organization. In late September 1973 the focus of SEATO activities shifted. SEATO's primary function became the assistance of security/development projects in Thailand and the Philippines.

wanted naval facilities and air bases including a new B-52 base. Tactical Air Wings and other units and activities employed in Vietnam, Laos, and Cambodia required logistical support facilities as well as bases. US foreign policy called for Thai combat units in Vietnam and Thai support generally for overall US policy and for activities in Thailand concerning Vietnam and the rest of Southeast Asia.[44] US efforts in behalf of Thai counterinsurgency must be viewed against the political background of negotiations to achieve larger scale US foreign policy objectives as well as in light of Thai concerns and aspirations.

(C) Organizing the in-country, US CI assistance effort to Thailand was primarily accomplished under Ambassador Graham Martin during his tour in Bangkok from 1963 to 1967. Ambassador Martin inherited leadership of a large US Mission administering a complex and expanding aid program that required the close cooperation of American agencies and their agents with counterpart Thai organizations and officials. The American development and CI assistance programs also had counterparts to the difficulties experienced by the Thai: bureaucratic red tape, politics, inter-agency rivalries, orientation to Bangkok, proliferation of programs, duplication of effort, overkill, lack of perception, inadequate intelligence, and more. Perception of the insurgent threat began to grow within the US mission generally and a crash development and CI assistance effort started in 1962. A fuller realization of the scope of the communist insurgency and the CI requirements began to emerge after the TPLAF armed attacks started in 1965, catching the Mission about as much by surprise as the RTG. The US attempts to support Thai CI requirements encompassed programs that started in the 1950s as well as those of the 1960s and included, but were not limited to, the following: (1) the US Operations Missions (USOM's) programs concerning economic, political, and social development, (2) the Military Assistance Programs (MAP) and advisory programs for the Royal Thai Armed Forces (RTARF) administered by the US Military Assistance Command, Thailand (MACTHAI) and the Joint US Military Advisory Group, Thailand (JUSMAGTHAI), (3) the civic action programs of the Thailand tenanted US forces involved in out-of-country actions, (4) US Information Service (USIS) programs, (5) ARPA's research and development efforts, and (6) the developmental contributions of US Army Support, Thailand (USARSUPTHAI). To coordinate direction of these US efforts under his command, Ambassador Martin created the Embassy post of the ambassador's Special Assistance for Counterinsurgency (SA/CI).[45]

(S) Ambassador Martin and the first two SA/CIs, Peer de Silva (1966-1968) and George K. Tanham (1968-1970), were of one mind on concepts for organizing US CI assistance. Martin insisted upon the ambassador's full authority in command and control of all Mission components; he did not believe in the country team, consensus approach to directing the Mission. Martin also insisted on firm control over US military contributions to Thai CI. He was dedicated to avoiding militarizing and Americanizing Thai CI as was done to CI in Vietnam. The US military were limited, with some exceptions, to advising senior Thai officers, training Thai military and paramilitary, and procuring military hardware. Peer de Silva, a former chief of the Central Intelligence Agency (CIA) station in Saigon, and his replacement, George Tanham, an I/CI specialist who had experienced a tour in Saigon, both strongly believed in unified management and civilian control of CI. When Ambassador Leonard Unger was posted to Bangkok in 1967, he essentially continued through 1973 the inherited Mission CI organization and policies: restrained US presence, unified civilian management, and limited US military involvement -- policies supported in Washington, at the Department of Defense, and by the Commander-in-Chief of the Pacific Command (CINCPAC), but not always as enthusiastically supported by the Commander of the US MACTHAI (COMUSMACTHAI).[46]

(S) US aid strategies and tactics evolved during the 1960s and early 1970s but the changes did not alter the main thrust of US Embassy policy, expounded and often refined in the Ambassador's "General Concept of US Support of Thai Counterinsurgency" and Tanham's "Guidelines."[47] The central principle has been to help the Thai help themselves, to act as a catalyst to bring about self-sustaining Thai initiative, management, training, funding, maintenance, and conduct of effective CI programs. Singled out for US help have been programs to help the Thai improve administration of local government, communications and information to remote areas, and motivation of Thai leadership. High priority programs have also been those involving rural living standards and security, to include improving intelligence collection and protection forces such as police, military, and militia. Specific points emphasized in the "Guidelines" include protecting US personnel, lines of communication, and bases; avoiding a client relationship and prolonged commitment of US resources; training Thai cadre to train Thai; the importance of coordinating the Thai CI effort and coordinating the Thai CI effort and coordinating assistance of the United States as well; prohibiting US personnel in Thai combat operations and at Thai headquarters below the battalion level and later the regimental level; minimizing the American presence, especially in sensitive border zones; proper processing of intelligence data; transferring program responsibility to the Thai as quickly as possible; and limiting the types and extent of US Military Civic Actions (MCA) activities (USAF MCA activities in Thailand were restricted to operations within a radius of 16 kilometers* from each base.) Thus, since the mid 1960s, there has been little doubt about the Ambassador's desires relative to US mission assistance to Thai CI.

US Military Contributions to Thai CI (U)

(C) US CI efforts in Thailand have involved the US military in three ways. First, under COMUSMACTHAI/JUSMAGTHAI, military hardware, advice, training, and certain other assistance have been provided Thailand to increase its CI capabilities. Second, US forces at six major Thai bases and several smaller installations, by establishing their security posture have augmented Thai CI capability. Third, increasingly, as the Embassy authorized deliberate exceptions to the policy of restrained US presence, certain US forces provided special developmental assistance as well as limited support to RTG CI operations. The mere presence of sizeable US forces in the underdeveloped Northeast might be a spur to economic development** and could also be included in US CI aid, but it was the RTG

---

* (S) Extensions to this limit were considered on a case by case basis by the US Embassy in Thailand.
** (U) The service industries around a military installation largely shut down when the installation closes. However, at least some of the capital put into the local economy by the military stays in the area as do some of the people educated and technically trained during the operation of the installation. The education and training more than the capital are the likely spurs to the local economy.

67

that limited the number of Americans in Thailand to those with jobs that Thai could not perform. Consequently, thousands of jobs have been provided the Thai directly by the US Government and many more indirectly by G.I. spending, but this situation is mostly by design of the RTG.[48]

(C) MACTHAI/JUSMAGTHAI is a subordinate unified command under the operational command of CINCPAC, and COMUSMACTHAI has operational control of and coordinating authority over assigned US forces and military agencies. COMUSMACTHAI is CINCPAC's single senior representative in Thailand, represents the Secretary of Defense with respect to MAP, and under the direction of the Ambassador who is Chief of Mission, coordinates US military affairs with other components of the US Mission. In addition to customary MAP, advisory, and technical assistance roles, MACTHAI/JUSMAGTHAI has been providing special in-country CI training using the US Army Special Forces Thailand and the 93rd Psychological Operations Detachment. Both of these US Army units were configured for their training roles and have been widely deployed in small teams to training sites throughout Thailand. MACTHAI also has a special intelligence analysis center for processing CI data, and MACTHAI's principal point of contact with the Embassy on CI matters is the J-3 staff which interfaces primarily with the Counselor of the Development and Security (DS) Section and the Political-Military (POMIL) Section.[49]

(C) Security for US forces at sites in Thailand has necessitated training Thai security guards and forming protection agreements between US commanders and local Thai political and military officials. Because the Embassy has assessed the insurgent threat to installations with US forces as low*

---

* (S) Attacks against US forces in Thailand have been the work of North Vietnamese Army (NVA) sapper teams which have received little support from the CPT.[50] CT attacks have been aimed exclusively at RTG or suspected RTG installations, units, and agents, and while the TPLAF has a high capability for attacking US tenanted bases, US intelligence agencies estimate the actual TPLAF threat to the bases to be low. The estimated threat from NVA sapper teams has varied from low to moderate -- mostly based upon the degree to which the United States was prosecuting the Southeast Asian fighting.

and because both the RTG and US policy is for a low US profile, the Embassy prohibits US security forces from firing weapons at points off the installation. Consequently, US forces have hired, trained, and equipped Thai to provide a large part of base security and have pushed for effective Thai reaction forces to provide beyond-the-perimeter security in conjunction with local CPM security forces. Further, in addition to other beneficial effects, the USAF MCA operations authorized within 16 kilometers of the base substantially enhanced the gathering of intelligence about possible attacks.[51] It should be stressed that authorization for MCA operations specifically excluded any US "nation-building" style activities without both Embassy and Thai approval, strongly urged that MCA be undertaken dually with a sponsoring RTG unit, and heavily stressed the goal of enhancing the RTG's image in the eyes of the people.[52] In addition to the around-base civic actions of the Thirteenth Air Force tenanted units, elements of USARSUPTHAI have conducted projects in the vicinity of their installations and the lines of communications they built and have been using to support US forces in Thailand.[53]

(C) By way of special CT developmental assistance to the Thai, the US Air Force conducted more far-reaching civic actions before directed to phase back to the 16 kilometer, non-nation building limit in 1969. The 606th Air Commando Squadron, the forerunner of the 56th Special Operations Wing, carried on direct, people-to-people medical, health education, construction, veterinary, on-the-job training, and other assistance to improve the living conditions of the people throughout the Northeast.[54] Construction units assigned to USARSUPTHAI and Navy SEABEE* units attached to USOM

---
* (U) US Navy Construction Battalion.

have built bases, communications systems, and roads in the Northeast and elsewhere since 1962.[55] The road networks have already assisted RTG developmental efforts and movement of CPM CI reaction forces. Many of the other facilities will be useful after the US forces have withdrawn. Direct support of Thai CI came from the US Air Force from March 1966 to January 1967. Twenty-five helicopters borrowed from Vietnam were flown in non-combat support of RTG CI operations so that CI momentum would not be lost while the Thai trained and organized to handle this airlift support job themselves.[56] All in all, the US military has played a minor role in Thai CI beyond supplying military equipment. The major role has fallen to the Thai themselves assisted largely by non-military components of the US Mission.

Contributions to Thai CI From Other Mission Components (U)

(S) The Ambassador and his DS and POMIL sections of the Embassy, USOM, USIS, ARPA, and the CIA have had the most impact on Thai CI although other components of the US Government have made contributions. Each main US contributor has had regional offices at various up-country locations. Embassy matters, for example, are handled by American Consuls at Udorn, Chiang Mai, and Songkhla. The Consuls are representatives of the Ambassador and are the senior US Government officials for CI matters in the respective regions.[57]

(U) USOM represents the US Agency for International Development (AID) and provides economic and technical assistance to the RTG primarily in the areas of economic, political, and social development. It and its forerunners have been in Thailand since 1950, and some two-thirds to three-quarters of its contributions have gone into RTG activities directly related to CI. It has supported major road building, health, aeronautical ground services, communications, police expansion, security, development, political awareness, governmental administration, agricultural assistance, and various training programs through the RTG Ministries, Departments, and Agencies which actually administer most of the aid. USOM has concentrated on helping the Thai improve their institutions and capabilities for coping with the requirements of CI and effective economic development.[58]

(U) USIS is the overseas arm of the United States Information Agency (USIA) and has been in Thailand since 1953. It has been supporting RTG programs to get information about RTG policies and developmental aid to the people, especially to villagers in remote rural areas. It has funded and provided informational programs for motion picture projection, radio, and television, written materials for distribution to libraries and to the people directly by the RTG, and has suggested mobile information teams for the RTG. USIS has also assisted USAF civic actions programs by, for example, providing printed materials designed to encourage villagers to inform the Thai police about suspicious activity near the USAF tenanted Air Bases.[59]

(U) ARPA, in the Office of the Secretary of Defense, has been responsible for establishing the joint Thai-US MRDC for the purpose of research, development, testing, and evaluation (RDTE) of activities in support of the RTARF. The emphasis has been on CI capabilities, increasing Thai appreciation for RDTE, increasing Thai ability to do RDTE, and gathering information in Thailand of use to the United States. Work undertaken by ARPA-MRDC included tactics, plans, equipment, development, and sociological, psychological, and human factors bearing on I/CI. Qualified scholars of many scientific disciplines have been conducting these analytical and developmental studies. Projects for the RTG produced an individual combat ration, several improved personal equipment items, a border control system, the Thailand Information Center, a CI System Manual, a shallow-draft boat evaluation, studies on insurgent operations and village life in rural Thailand, and many other direct contributions to development, security, and CI. MRDC has evolved into an essentially Thai enterprise under the command and control of the Supreme Command although it receives aid from US and other sources.[60] The various ARPA and MRDC sponsored histories concerned with Thai-US efforts relative to I/CI in Thailand have been invaluable in preparing this report.

(C) Turbulence occurred in US mission CI efforts just as it did in the Thai efforts and for many of the same kinds of reasons. For example, Ambassador Martin in 1965 directed the CIA to sponsor the BPP which it did to good effect into 1967 and 1968. By 1969, however, the BPP dropped from the elite paramilitary CI force it had been because the RTA took exception to growing BPP prestige and the CIA had phased out its sponsorship during 1967 and 1968 at the direction of the main CIA office in Washington. This type of program command direct from Washington made the Ambassador's single-manager control of US mission CI efforts somewhat illusory. Not only were programs taken off the shelf and applied with little or no tailoring to the Thai situation, but also the directors in country were responsible to their agency heads in Washington for the spending of allocated funds. The Ambassador had no authority to switch funding from one project to another and no counterpart agency for CI in Washington to which to appeal.[61] Congress also was erratic in its support of the AID program generally and during the early 1970s increasingly attacked the CI efforts and CI funding of ARPA.[62] Under these sorts of control handicaps, the Ambassador has coordinated the CI efforts of the Mission as best he could while pursuing a pilot-program, trial-and-error, learning course much as the Thai have been doing.

CHAPTER VI
CONCLUSION (U)

(C) There were neither prepared programs nor rules to follow in either creating the insurgency or developing the counterinsurgency in Thailand. Essentially, the CTs, the RTG, and the US Mission all relied on general guidelines and trial and error to shape actions that usually were tested in pilot programs. The insurgents have apparently had very effective planning and to all indications have executed their programs reasonably well. In contrast, the RTG and the US Mission, while planning well, have not enjoyed the same degree of effective program implementation due to bureaucracy, interagency competition, and attempts to use methodology developed for other times, other places, and other peoples.

(C) The Thai people have a complex society that hinders, if not prevents, rapid initiation of any revolutionary program. The insurgent recruiters play on the conservatism and lack of political awareness of the people. Targeted groups receive promises of an unchanged but better operating social system, help with their immediate problems, and large amounts of personal attention. Thai acceptance of most things that will not cause problems and avoidance of anything foreign and controversial enables initial insurgent contacts, but mitigates against indoctrination with communism. The RTG is at a disadvantage in countering insurgent appeals and inroads because of the very personal and flexible insurgent approach, the paucity of intelligence and its analysis, the revolutionary appearance of the RTG developmental programs, and the history of special privilege for RTG officials. Historically, the RTG has also been a conservative entity where power blocs shared government and its fruits -- further making a unified, efficient CI effort difficult to produce despite intentions.

(C) Protagonists in Thai I/CI have a variety of complex intentions, and their future actions appear to be quite conditional and intertwined. The Thai have a heritage of protecting their national identity from foreign influences and this, along with national political stability and economic development, will probably command a higher priority than CT suppression. US intentions include keeping bases in Thailand, stopping the expanding influence of communist powers, and enhancing US influence in Asia and the world. The Soviet Union (USSR) and the Democratic Republic of Vietnam apparently intend to enlarge their influence in Southeast Asia and in Thailand, moves which China apparently intends to counter. The CPT and Thai insurgents intend to take political power from the RTG, but outside support that the insurgents will continue to need is tied to regional and world politics and will oscillate with international political maneuvering. The DRV and the USSR will most likely continue to probe for influence positions and actively support the insurgents in Thailand. China will likely oppose USSR and DRV expansionist efforts by covertly agreeing to a continued American presence in Thailand and Southeast Asia and by increasing its ties as well as influence with the RTG. China likely will also, at least temporarily, cool its materiel support to the CPT and TPLAF without relinquishing any influence and offer other enticements to return Thailand more firmly under Chinese suzerainty. The RTG will be apt, with the understanding of China and the United States, ostensibly to insist upon reducing US influence and US military forces in Thailand, to initiate closer ties

FIGURE 14

with China, and to jockey for the optimum position for Thailand vis a vis China, Vietnam, the Soviet Union, the United States, and other international forces. The prime internal concern of the RTG will remain governmental stability with economic development a possible second and with counterinsurgency having a third or lower priority. Additionally, because the student riots of October 1973 resulted in the ouster of Thanom and Prapass, the RTG and its positions will be in somewhat of a flux for a time, and insurgency is apt to expand.

EPILOG

(U) Thai newspaper articles at the turn of the year 1973-1974 suggest that Thai international politics and CI are in such a state of flux. On 29 December 1973 when Deputy Foreign Minister Chatichai Choonavan left Peking, the Bangkok Post proclaimed in banner headlines, "Peking throws the door wide open -- Six month's supply of diesel fuel (at a special friendship price), two-way trade, US pull-out rate satisfactory." The article went on to say,

> ....Prime Minister Chou En-Lai did not ask for quick withdrawal of American troops stationed in Thailand... General Chatichai was deeply impressed by Peking's peaceful intentions...Premier Chou said that Soviet strategy today was worse than during the time of Peter the Great because the Soviet fleet had come to the Indian Ocean...

On 4 January 1974 in front page headlines, the Bangkok Post reported, "Govt to end CSOC, reallocate budget" and added that, "...The word 'Communist' is to be taken off the name of any successor to CSOC because it will deal with all types of insurgency, not only Communism..." By 5 January 1974, the Bangkok Post's front page read:

>Army takes over from CSOC, the National Security Council yesterday decided to reorganize this country's communist suppression activities...turning over armed suppression activities to the army under control of the Ministry of Defense...the army will operate in the most sensitive areas to supplement police forces under the Ministry of Interior. Police forces will be reassigned as normal functions of various ministries. The National Security Council meeting was chaired by Prime Minister Prof Sanya Dharmsakti. Counterinsurgency operations will be coordinated through a unit in the Prime Minister's Office and under the direction of the Prime Minister...

And, in the feature story of the Bangkok Post Sunday Magazine, 6 January 1974, John Burgess at Km 48, Pakse -- Paksong Highway, Laos reports on:

> Face to Face -- The barbed-wire curtain -- Where Thai and North Vietnamese troops are building a cautious trust founded in the ceasefire in Laos (and where) a shoulder-high barrier of wood and barbed wire is all that separates a Thai and a Vietnamese army dug in opposite each other here on the lush Boloven Plateau...[63]

(U) Long term trends appear to be established, while shorter range maneuvering and timing are less predictable.

Udorn, Thailand
January 1974

APPENDIX A

J-2 USMACTHAI/JUSMAGTHAI
THAILAND THREAT BRIEF
10 January 1974

INTRODUCTION

(U) The Kingdom of Thailand, formerly known as Siam, is located in the heart of mainland Southeast Asia. It has an area about the size of Wyoming and Colorado combined. Thailand has common boundaries with Burma on the west and north, Laos on the north and east, Cambodia on the southeast, and Malaysia on the south.

(U) Thailand's topography is diversified. There are four main geographic regions -- North, Northeast, Central, and South:

Northern Thailand is primarily a region of mountains and valleys which comprises about one-quarter of the total land area. The mountains, running north and south, are forested, and the valleys between them are narrow and fertile.

The Northeast Region, a large plateau (the Korat Plateau), rising about 1,000 feet above the central plain, comprises roughly one-third of the country. A great deal of this land is of poor soil quality and suffers from occasional droughts or floods depending on the season.

The Central Region is dominated by Thailand's most important river, the Chao Phraya. The land is rich in alluvium and watered by an extensive network of canals and irrigation projects.

The Southern Region, a long sliver of land extending from central Thailand south to Malaysia, is covered in great part by rain forest.

(U) The climate of much of the country is dominated by monsoons. In most regions there are three seasons: rainy (June-October), cool (November-February), and hot (March-May). Rainfall varies but is generally heaviest in the South and lightest in the Northeast.

(U) Thailand's population of an estimated 40 million is composed primarily of people of Thai stock. The principal minority groups are an estimated two million ethnic Chinese located in the larger urban areas, about 800,000 Malay-speaking Moslems in the southernmost provinces; the various hill tribes in the North (estimated at about 286,000); and 45,000 Vietnamese refugees, mostly in the Northeast. Bangkok, the capital, and its environs has about 3.8 million inhabitants, according to a 1972 estimate. Although the population of Bangkok forms the economic head of the Thai political body, Thailand remains a predominantly rural country with the majority of the population living in the non-municipal areas.

(U) Since 1947 the urban population has been growing faster than the rural population. The difference between rural and urban growth rates is the imbalance of migration between the two sectors; migration is streaming toward the cities and away from the land resulting in highly congested areas such as Bangkok and fraught with all the urban problems found elsewhere in the world. One of the major socio-economic and political problems facing Thailand stems from an estimated seven million households with only 700,000 having money to spare for anything but the bare necessities of life.

(U) The Communist Party of Thailand (CPT), established in 1942, has advocated armed revolution since 1952. Communist infiltration and subversion began secretly as early as 1959, with the actual decision to start organizing the insurgency made in 1961, and was brought into the open in 1965 with armed insurgent attacks on Thai security forces and systematic assassinations of loyal village leaders in Northeast Thailand, the country's poorest region. In 1967 insurgency broke out in the North, where communist agents had begun recruitment among Meo hill tribesmen as early as 1959. The communist have also attempted, with some success, to establish typical front groups in areas primarily under party control of farmers, women, and youth. There may be a return to urban front organizations in the new political environment.

(C) The insurgency today is on the periphery of the Thai society and its growth continues at a low level on a long continuum. It still remains a loosely-coordinated movement in the North, Northeast, Central, and Southern Regions -- each with markedly different characteristics. Whereas the insurgency in the more rugged Northern Region marks the most serious military threat to the Royal Thai Government (RTG), the Northeast communists have accomplished significant, although not continuous political growth in some of the mountainous areas of the Korat Plateau. Communists in the North and Northeast have benefited from abundant material support from the People's Republic of China (PRC) but primarily from the Democratic Republic of Vietnam (DRV). More limited external support and more aggressive RTG counterinsurgency efforts, particularly civic actions and psychological operations, have affected progress of the communists in the Central and Southern Regions of Thailand.

(C) With the exception of the Northern Region, which has reported a significant decrease in the number of incidents reported in 1973 as compared to 1972, the remainder of the regional insurgencies in Thailand continue to show an increase in the number of incidents reported with the level of violence in these individual incidents more intense for the past year.

Armed insurgent strength has increased; in 1966 there were 1,200 Communist Terrorists (CT) within Thailand and an additional 600 insurgents of the Communist Terrorist Organization in the far South. Currently the CT have increased their numbers to nearly 6,300 armed full-time insurgents; however, caution should be used in using absolute figures inasmuch as all strength estimates are derived from rough RTG data. This 6,300 does not include 800-900 poorly armed village militia in the North and an additional 4,000-5,000 unarmed village militia in the Northeast. In seven years the CTO in the far South have nearly quadrupled to 2,200.

(C) Information used in examining the insurgency comes primarily from Thai sources and is obtained from reports; discussions with other US Mission agencies, third country nationals; and local news media. As a result, the possibility exists that some of this information may have been provided to us to further the national aims and objectives of the Royal Thai Government. We do believe, however, that information, to include statistics, on the insurgency in Thailand will continue to be a good estimate of the situation.

(C) An analysis of the insurgency requires an examination of a combination of factors and not from any one single aspect. The following are some of the factors which we believe presently influence the interpretation and priority of insurgency:

1. Tactics and techniques of the insurgents, to include military, political, socio-economic, and psychological.

2. External influences and outside aid, such as material and propaganda, to the insurgency and recent raproachment with China.

3. Level of CT military and organizational activity.

4. RTG and CT casualty figures.

5. CT strength figures.

6. Dimensions of areas of significant communist presence.

7. Political and socio-economic instability, such as: labor and youth movements; inflation; rice and petroleum shortages; reduction in US aid; government reorganization and increased nationalism which leads to continued public apathy toward the supposedly more remote insurgency and a diversion of RTG efforts.

8. Criminal acts which appear to be insurgent activities from information reported.

NORTH THAILAND

(C) In North Thailand, the communist insurgents have been able to consolidate their past military victories and effectively control large areas of remote mountainous terrain. Provinces most susceptible to communist influence are: Chiang Rai, Nan, Uttaradit, Tak, and the Tri-province area of Phetchabun, Phitsanulok and Dan Sai District, Loei. The armed insurgent strength in the area is currently estimated at approximately 2,450 to 2,550, plus an additional 800-900 armed village militia. The insurgent force in the Northern Region is comprised primarily of hilltribesmen with ethnic and Sino-Thai providing most of the trained cadre and leadership. Although many attempts have been made, the insurgents have not been successful in gaining mass support from the ethnic lowland Thais. This, in addition to the relatively small hilltribe population, presents serious limitations to insurgent expansion efforts; however, it is possible that the Northern insurgents may attempt to increase their recruitment of Laotian hilltribes, and may even seek increased support from the Pathet Lao.

(C) The Communist Party of Thailand's Northern Regional Headquarters controls all insurgent military and organizational activity in the area. This is believed to be a mobile headquarters, moving between Pua District, Nan, and Sayaboury Province of Laos. Subordinate to the Northern Regional Headquarters, the insurgents have established individual area command headquarters in their principal operating areas in Chiang Rai, Nan and the Tri-province area. These area commands provide overall guidance to the insurgent activities in their respective areas.

(C) The insurgents in the North have not yet organized themselves into formal battalions and regiments, and instead are classified into two separate categories: the regular force soldier of the Thai Peoples' Liberation Armed Forces and the village militia. Although the Northern insurgents are capable of mustering company-size forces for specific objectives, their normal operating strength is as platoon and squad size units. The village militia units, normally ranging in size from five to ten men each, are responsible for population control and protection of the village. On occasion, however, these units are organized and used to augment the regular force units for specific operations.

(C) The regular force units are currently armed with modern US, but principally Chinese weapons. These include rifles and carbines, as well as automatic weapons and a limited number of crew served weapons. During the fall and winter of 72-73, it is estimated that the CPT probably infiltrated enough individual weapons to fully rearm the entire Northern CT force. During the recently completed joint force training exercise 17, conducted from 1 November 1973 to 6 January 1974, the CT in the mountainous areas of Phu Rang Ka in western Chiang Rai Province and Doi Pha Chi in southeastern Chiang Rai and northwestern Nan lost large quantities of food supplies. It is estimated JFTX-17 forces captured or destroyed enough provisions to sustain a CT force of more than 250 men for 12 months, with one report stating approximately 36 tons of rice had been seized in the last phase of the exercise.

(C) The insurgents in Tak Province, and the village militia throughout the North, are armed primarily with US World War II vintage weapons and locally procured weapons, such as shotguns and flintlocks. Some of the village militia are currently arming themselves with captured M-16s and M-79 grenade launchers. Because of an increased dependence on Chinese and Soviet weapons, the insurgents continue to require more external logistical support. As a result, they have created a primitive, but effective, logistical system to infiltrate these weapons into the country. All of this material is brought into Northern Thailand by either porters or pack animals from major supply depots located in Sayaboury and Luang Prabang Provinces of Laos.

(C) During recent years, the CPT has taken various steps to increase their political and military influence in Northern Thailand. Selected cadre and many young tribesmen, both male and female, have received advanced political and military training from communist school[s] in Laos, North Vietnam, and China. In addition to training and materiel, the Northern insurgents have also received manpower support from out-of-country sources. Approximately 200 red Chinese soldiers, including a small number of Han Chinese, from Yunnan Province, China, continue to operate with the Thai insurgents in Chiang Rai, Nan, and the Tri-province area. Although some of these Chinese are acting as advisors, the majority have reportedly been integrated into TPLAF line squads. The Northern Regional Headquarters has also received limited support from Northeastern Thailand. A small number of Northeastern insurgents, highly skilled in political and organizational work, are now operating in Northern Thailand with the explicit mission of organizing a political support structure in the area.

(C) To date, the CT have been very successful in halting RTG road building through insurgent operating areas in Northern Thailand, primarily in Tak, Chiang Rai, and Nan Provinces. We believe the insurgents in the area consider the construction of new roads as a threat to their freedom of movement as successful completion of construction efforts would enhance the image of the RTG, reduce insurgent control of the local populace, and reduce CT credibility.

NORTHEAST THAILAND

(C) The CPT in Northeast Thailand potentially offer the RTG its most serious problems in counterinsurgency -- in that the CPT there has geared itself to a protracted political struggle modeled ideally after the teachings of Mao-Tse-Tung. Greater amounts of landspace and village populace are controlled by the CPT in the Northeast than in other regions; political control over these people is likewise more advanced than corresponding CPT influence in North, Central, or South Thailand. This influence extends to roughly one percent of the total Northeast population, but several socio-economic factors now exist which could provide a recruit support base for the CPT and sympathetic support to their ideology. Among these factors are: (1) the land generally is of poor soil quality, thus making inhabitants the poorest in comparison to those of other regions; (2) government indifference or inability to demonstrate sufficient attention to the problems common to villagers (a problem common to North Thailand as well); and (3) feeling in some circles of government that the Northeastern Thai are more akin to Lao than Central Thai, further emphasizing this government indifference, apparent or otherwise. These reasons, coupled with what most observers see as increasing logistical support from the NVA and Pathet Lao, could seriously hamper RTG counterinsurgency projects in the area, particularly in and around areas now under CPT influence.

(C) Armed insurgents, that is the full-time jungle soldiers, now number in excess of 2,300 which is a 54 percent increase over 1971 estimates, and does not include recent recruiting in southern Ubon and western Udorn. More than half of these 2,300 full-time soldiers are located in and around

Na Kae District, Nakhon Phanom, which continues to be the most politically advanced area in Thailand.

(C) The Na Kae organization is part of the CPT Nakhon Phanom Provincial Committee, which is one of five provincial-level committees subordinate to the Northeast Central Committee. The headquarters for the Northeast Central Committee is also reported to be located in Na Kae District. Besides the NKP Committee, the Sakon Nakhon Committee controls parts of Nong Khai, Sakon Nakhon, and Kalasin, and the Udorn Committee is responsible for large and expanding areas of western Udorn and eastern and northern Loei Provinces. Provincial-level committees in the mountainous border areas in Korat-Buriram-Prachinburi and southern Ubon, and a small recruiting group in Surin and Sisaket, are under headquarters 303, the CPT southern branch of the Northeast Central Committee. The exact relationship between the Central Committee and Headquarters 303 is not well-defined at this time.

(C) Although the jungle force in NKP and Sakon Nakhon is organized into main force and local force structures, virtually everyone is responsible for food collection activities and masses' development work. Several recent defectors from the NKP-Sakon Nakhon area have complained about serious food shortages, pointing up that the CPT may be having trouble in keeping its village support mechanisms satisfied in the face of increased RTG military presence. Recently there is evidence that the purported CI efforts in Na Kae District in that past have in fact been negligible contributing to the credibility of the CT and increasing their support base.

(C) In addition to the full-time jungle strength, the CPT has recruited an estimated 5,000 village militia members and formed them into village militia units (VMUs). Almost all of these VMUs are in NKP alone. There are still no indications that these VMUs are being individually armed other than for short periods of time, usually when participating in military actions alongside regular force soldiers. These VMUs support this regular force by carrying out acts of terrorism and supply collection as well as serving as a source for regular force emplacements.

(C) Weaponry is obtained in a number of ways. A large quantity of Chinese and Soviet ammunition, small arms, automatic weapons, light mortars, and RPG-2s are brought into Thailand by party cadre as well as scheduled arms shipments from North Vietnam. US-manufactured small arms, M-16s and M-79s captured from RTG forces are also used in tactical operations. Some weapons are supplied by groups or individuals solely for profit. No reports have been received of more sophisticated weapons, such as: 75mm recoilless rifles, 107mm, 122mm, or 140mm rockets having been transported across the Thai border, however, the possibility of Thai insurgents having these weapons should not be discounted.

(C) The biggest worries for the RTG in the Northeast now are the increased aid from North Vietnam and Laos since the Vietnam ceasefire, and the willingness of the CPT to take its time and appear dormant while strengthening its political base in and around their ever-expanding operating areas.

CENTRAL THAILAND

(C) From a communist insurgency viewpoint, Central Thailand (primarily four remote valleys) remains the least active, probably due to the relative prosperity. The recent student inspired insurrection which brought about the collapse of the Thanom-Prapass government in October 1973 has created a large socio-economic and political upheaval in Central Thailand which has spread throughout the country. It was not a communist inspired insurrection, although there are indications the CPT are attempting to infiltrate and influence this movement.

(C) Other reports concerning Khmer insurgent (KI) activities indicate intentions to conduct subversive activities in Chanthaburi and Trat Provinces, Thailand, and reportedly a group of KI have crossed into Thailand for these purposes. Other areas of the East Central Region have been quiet.

(C) The western fringes of the Central Region are less prosperous and the Communists' promises of a "good life" are more readily believed, and in these areas the insurgency continues to develop. CT strength in the region is estimated at 150-190 armed soldiers and approximately 750-950 supporters and sympathizers. These CT operate in Rat Buri, Phet Buri, and Prachuap Khiri Khan Provinces. In the mountain areas of the west, where CT sightings have increased substantially in the last six months, the insurgents are primarily Karens, with only a few low-landers. The insurgents of Rat Buri province are armed with M-16s, World War II vintage US small arms and locally procured shotguns. In Phet Buri Province weapons consist of World War II vintage weapons of US origin (mostly carbines) and locally procured weapons. In Prachuap Khiri Khan insurgents are armed with M-16s, shotguns, World War II vintage weapons, and some M-79 grenade launchers have also been reported. Also recently the CT have been reported having radios in their possession in this area.

SOUTH THAILAND

(C) In the South the problem of active subversion is small compared to that of the North and Northeast Regions, but of nearly equal intensity, and it is this region where we have identified three different insurgencies: Communist Terrorist (CT) of the CPT; Communist Terrorist Organization (CTO) of the Communist Party of Malaysia (CPM); and the Muslim Separatist Movement.

(C) The CT of the CPT operating in the mountain range that divides the Kra Peninsula number approximately 1,050 and are controlled by the Southern Regional Central Committee -- believed to be located in the Phatthalung/Trang Provincial border area. These insurgents remain deployed in small permanent base camps with support and training facilities, with normal combat missions conducted by squad or platoon size elements operating as independent units. The CT of the South continue to receive the majority of their food and financial support from local sources, but RTG civic actions coupled with psychological operations are making it difficult for these supplies to reach the jungle soldiers.

(C) During the past six months the CT in Nakhon Si Thammarat, Surat Thani, Phatthalung, Trang, Krabi, Satun, and Songkhla have expanded their influence, probably due to reduced RTG military counterinsurgency efforts, and extended their activity further south, possibly due to an agreement with the CTO. It was also reported during this period that several high ranking male members were expelled from the CPT because of attempts to force their affections on female cadre. Also, many low-level members have defected recently complaining of the hard life and stating they have lost faith in the communist promises. However, it is possible that these defections are due to the communist hopes of winning at the polls what they have been unable to do militarily.

(C) The CTO -- the military arm of the Communist Party of Malaysia -- has used the five southern border provinces of Thailand as a refuge and support base since the early days of the Malaysian Emergency (1958-60). Although the stated CPM main objective is Malaysia, there is no evidence that the CTO intend to relinquish their presently controlled areas within the Thai border. Today the CTO have rebuilt their organization and are currently estimated to have an armed strength of 2,200, operating primarily in Songkhla, Yala, and Narathiwat Provinces. In addition to this main jungle force, the Malaysia Communist Youth League has a membership of about 3,000, who support the CTO and a number of whom are annually recruited into the four regiments of the CTO. Recently reports indicate a serious ethnic disagreement between two of these CTO regiments: the 8th (composed of Malay/Thai) and the 12th (composed of Malay/Chinese). If a split does occur, the 8th CTO regiment might well join forces with the CPT.

(C) The ethnic make-up of the Far South is mostly Malay/Thai and helps explain the strength of the third identified insurgency, the Separatist Movement, which is centered in Pattani and extending into parts of Northern Narathiwat Province. These Malay speaking Muslim-Separatist have an estimated armed strength of 250-300, and have become more vigorous in clamoring for the creation of their own sovereignty.

(C) Armament of the insurgents in the Southern Region consist primarily of World War II vintage weapons, both of US and British origin, however, an increasing number of AK-47s, M-16s, and M-79 grenade launchers have also been reported to be in the hands of these insurgents. And the CTO reportedly are manufacturing their own ammunition for the M-79 grenade launchers.

(C) Strength estimates provided for the CTO and Muslim Separatist have not and are not coordinated figures, as neither movement is considered a threat to the sovereignty of Thailand by RTG authorities.

CONCLUSION

(C) In conclusion, the communist inspired insurgencies remain small, vulnerable and, for the most part, limited to the periphery of the Thai nation and society. There is no charismatic leadership for either the regional insurgencies or the Communist Party of Thailand, and the jungle forces are not organized into conventionally identifiable units, e.g., companies or battalions, in the North they are identified as "area commands," Northeast as "regions," "units" in Central Thailand, and "camps" in the South, with "regiments" belonging to the CTO. Taking into consideration present RTG counterinsurgency efforts, we estimate that the communist inspired insurgencies will continue to grow throughout Thailand. Insurgent groups will continue to expand in number, intensify their actions, and as in the past continue to expand their areas of operations. They are also expected to develop a more sophisticated command and control organization, and upgrade their weaponry as more communist weapons and materials are infiltrated into Thailand. Reports during the past six-nine months clearly indicate that Hanoi is placing greater emphasis on support to the Thai insurgency by increased training of insurgents, materiel support, and improved transportation methods.

(C) Furthermore, the Communist(s probably have the capability to penetrate almost any of the fixed installations within Thailand for periods of short duration and at times of their own choosing. The probability that the CPT has made or will make the decision, in the immediate future, to attack US-tenanted installations appears unlikely, but the possibility should not be discounted.

(C) For additional information, it should also be noted that all aircraft departing or entering airbases in Thailand and low flying aircraft anywhere in Thailand are particularly vulnerable to attack by such lightweight compact weapon systems as the AT-3 (Sagger) and SA-7 (Strella). None of these weapons systems are known to be in the hands of Thai based insurgents, but again this possibility should not be discounted.

APPENDIX B

IMPORTANT DATES IN THAI HISTORY THROUGH 1963

IMPORTANT DATES IN THAI HISTORY THROUGH 1963

6th Century, B.C.	Life of Buddha.
7th Century, A.D.	Mon Kingdom, Dvaravati (Central Thailand). Thai Kingdom, Nanchao, Yunnan (S.W. China).
11-12th Centuries	Thai tribes migrate south; zenith of Khmer Empire (Cambodia, Thailand).
1113-50	Suryavarman II, founder of Angkor Wat.
1253	Kublai Khan conquers Nanchao.
1283-1317	Rama Kamheng, King of Sukhotai, originates Thai alphabet, sends mission to Emperor of China.

AYUTHAYA PERIOD

1350	Founding of Ayuthaya.
1448-88	King Trailok, administrative and legal reforms.
1518	Portuguese mission to Ayuthaya.
1569	Burmese capture Ayuthaya.
1590-1605	King Naresuen kills Burmese Crown Prince, suzerain over Cambodia.
1605-10	King Ekatosarot: Japanese mercenaries (Yarnada, captain of the King's bodyguard); Netherland's factory.
1612	East India Company factories.
1657-88	King Narai, poet, patron of letters.
1685	Mission of Louis XIV (Chevalier de Chaumont).
1688	Phaulkon executed, death of King Narai, French expelled.
1767	Burmese destroy Ayuthaya: General Taksin repels Burmese King (at Thonburi).
1778	Capture of Vientiane, Emerald Buddha taken at Siam.
1782	General Chakri proclaimed King (Bangkok); Taksin executed.

BANGKOK PERIOD

1785-87	Nguyen Anh (later Emperor Gialong of Vietnam) in Bangkok.
1788	Buddhist Council revises canon.
1805-08	Revision of Law Code.
1824-26	First Anglo-Burmese War (ends Burmese threat to Siam).
1827	Lao Prince revolts; Thais occupy Vientiane.
1835	First printing press set up by American missionaries.
1837	Reformed Buddhist sect founded by Prince Mongkut.
1839-42	British defeat China in Opium War (deep effect on Siam).
1851	Accession of King Mongkut.
1855	Bowring Treaty of Friendship and Commerce (British trade, extra-territorial concessions): 'a total revolution in all the financial machinery of the Government', Sir J. Bowring.
1856-68	Treaties with France, USA, Denmark, Portugal, Netherlands, Prussia, Belgium, Italy, etc.

1868	Accession of King Chulalongkorn.
1874-1905	Abolition of slavery.
1880s	End of traditional junk trade with China; European steamers predominant.
1892-99	Rolyn Jacquemins (former Minister of Interior, Belgium) General Adviser to the King.
1893	French gunboats blockade Bangkok; Luang Prabang ceded to France.
1894-97	Criminal and Civil Courts established.
1896	Bangkok-Ayuthaya railway (1900 to Korat, 1921 to Chiangmai, 1922 link with Malaya)
1901	First Thai budget.
1903	Van der Heide's twelve-year irrigation plan shelved.
1907	Angkor Wat, four provinces ceded to France.
1908	Land Act: right to as much as each can use (eight to twenty acres): Founding of Chinese Chamber of Commerce
1909	Four Malay sultanates renounced.
1910	King Vajiravud, Failure of Chinese general strike, War against Germany. Chulalongkorn University founded.
1921	Compulsory education decreed.
1923	Earliest record of Communist activities in Thailand; some six CCP members, including Lin Hsueh and Chen Hsing-tai, sent from Shanghai to subvert Chinese minority.
1925	King Prajadiphok. Ho Chi Minh sent team to Thailand from Vietnam Revolutionary League based in Canton to set up small-scale cells among Vietnamese minority in the North-East. In late 1920s Ho himself lived in the North-East as Communist organizer for about two years, and in 1929 he created the "Overseas Vietnamese Association for the Salvation of the Fatherland."
1926	CCP formed a "South Seas Committee," which in 1927 changed to South Seas Communist Party, for purpose of conducting liaison with "revolutionary" groups in South-East Asia, including Indo-China, Burma, Thailand, Malaya, and Indonesia.
1927	Communist Youth of Siam established (in 1932 claimed 2,000 members, almost all Chinese).
1930	South Seas Communist Party dissolved; Comintern in April decided that Malayan Communist Party would be responsible for Communists in Malaya and Siam.
1932	"Communist Party of Siam" (CPS) and Youth Movement issued manifesto in Chinese.
1932	Promoters' Coup: End of Absolute Monarchy People's Party (Coup Group) coup; Constitutional Monarchy established by Provisional Constitution. Phraya Mano government. First permanent constitution.
1933	Mano given dictatorial powers. People's Party counter-coup (Mano and other conservatives arrested).

1933	Phraya Pabon government. Prince Boworadet led troops against Bangkok to restore absolute monarchy; revolt crushed by Army under Phibun Songkhram. Thai Government enacted anti-Communist legislation, i.e., against Communist Chinese in Thailand. General election.
1934	Communist Youth of Siam claimed 8 branches, and only 41 members.
1935	King Prachatipok abdicated; succeeded by his 16 year old nephew, King Ananda, under a regency. CPS announced opposition to "imperialism" and "feudalism." CPS represented at 7th Comintern. (Most sources consider 1935 to be year Communist Party first established in Siam, but some give the year 1929).
1936	First overt Communist demonstration at Khon Kaen.
1937	General election.
1938	General election. Pahon resigned after vote of no-confidence; succeeded by Phibun.
1939	Pro-monarchist plot led by Phraya Song Suradet discovered; 20 executed without trial. Restrictions on Chinese
1941	Alliance with Japan, seizure of parts of Burma, Laos and Cambodia.
1942	Communist Party of Thailand (CPT) held First Congress, but CPT remained underground during World War II; some of its members worked with the "Free Thai."
1942-43	Construction of 'death railway' to Burma.
1944	Phibun resigned. Pridi in power. Return of seized territories (1944-46).
(1944-47)	Pridi Phanomyong, dominant power.
1944	Khuang Apaiwong government.
1945	Thawi Bunyakhet government.
1946	General election. Khuang Apaiwong government. Pridi government. Revised constitution. Death of King Ananda, succeeded by brother, Bhumiphon. Admiral Thamrong Nawaset government Thai Government for the first time established diplomatic relations with China, but Thai envoy recalled in November 1947 (relation with the Republic of China were re-activated in 1949 at ministerial level; elevated to ambassadorial level 1958). Central Labour Union (CLU), created under CCPT and CPT directives, established and claimed to represent 51 unions; almost entirely Chinese in membership. CLU joined WFTU in 1949 but was dissolved in early 1950s

	Anti-Communist Act of 1933 revoked in October.
CPT emerged from illegality December 6 under leadership of Prasert Sapsunthorn, Member of Parliament (MP), claiming vastly exaggerated membership of 50,000; published Masses Weekly.
"Ten Principles of the CPT which Members should Know" published and distributed in Thailand.
1947	November: Army coup restores Pibun. Pridi flees. (Coup by Army Coup Group-Phibun supporters); provisional constitution.
Khuang Apaiwong government.
CCPT and CPT joined in forming All-Thai Federation of Workers. Phibun Government arrested many Communists and the CPT went underground, November.
South-East Asian Communist Parties said to have held Conference at Udorn (Burmese, Thai, Vietnamese, Malayan, and Indonesian Parties) under chairmanship of Prince Souphanouvong.
1948	General election.
Army Coup Group forced Khuang to resign.
Phibun government.
Attempted coup by Army General Staff.
Phibun Government set up Thai National Trade Union Conference which joined the International Confederation of Free Trade Unions in 1950.
South-East Asia (Communist) Youth Conference held in Calcutta, February, was signal for strategy of militant insurrection in South and South-East Asia.
Soviet Union established Legation in Bangkok, May 4.
1949	Attempted coup by Pridi, Marines, Navy elements; put down by Army led by Gen. Sarit Thanarat.
New constitution by Army Coup Group.
Chinese immigration quota reduced to 200 a year.
At Peking Trade Union Conference of Asian and Australasian Countries, November, Liu Shao-Chi promoted revolution by armed struggle, wars of "national liberation."
CPT re-activated with Communist take-over of China; claimed 12,000 members and 100,000 sympathizers.
1950	US military and economic aid agreement.
1951	June: Navy revolt; three days fighting. November: 'Insiders' Coup'; Phao Dep. Minister of Interior, Sarit Dep. Minister of Defence.
Attempted coup by Navy and some Free Thais ("Manhattan" Incident); put down by Army, police, Air Force.
Insiders' (or "Radia") coup by Army and police.
King Bhumiphon took up duties.
CPR set up at Kunming "National Minorities Institute" for indoctrination of Thai Yi, Lolo, and other Yunnan ethnic groups.

1952	Modified 1932 Constitution reinstated. General election. Anti-Communist Act. "Un-Thai Activities" (anti-Communist) Act passed November by National Assembly; Kularb Saipradit and others arrested (Kularb later convicted of conspiracy); several hundred Communist Chinese deported. CPT Second Congress held and Central Committee formed.
1952-54	Communist plots, arrests, especially of Chinese.
1953	CPT announced formation of "Thai People's Autonomous Region in South Yunnan," January 31.
1954	In Peking broadcast Pridi Phanomyong appealed to Thai people to revolt against "American imperialism and its puppet, the Government of Thailand."
1954-55	CPT renewed almost open activities following the Geneva Conference on Indo-China and especially after the First Bandung Conference. Thai Government imposed martial law on North-East Provinces. Government banned imports from CPR.
1955	April-June: Pibun's world tour: 'democracy'. SEATO Headquarters established. Imports from China allowed.
1956	CPT sent greetings to CCP 8th Congress, September.
1957	February: controlled elections. September 16: Pibun and Phao ousted. December: Pote Sarasin caretaker Government. December 15: elections. General Thanom Prime Minister. General election. Sarit coup; Phibun and Phao went into exile. Pote Sarasin government (Interim). General election. CPT New Year Message called for united front to ward off threat of US "imperialism" to Thai independence (NCNA, January 25). "New Left" emerged with 1957 elections, later forming "Socialist Front" under Thep Chotinuchit, MP from North-East. "Peace fighter" presented candidates as "independents" in December elections. Government measures against CPT forced Party underground once more.
1958	Thanom Kittikachorn ("Caretaker") government. March: Twenty-six by-elections (Democrats win fourteen). July: US 'Friendship Highway', Saraburi to Korat, opened. October 20: Sarit's Revolution; martial law, Constitution abolished, parliament dissolved, Communists arrested. November: dispute with Cambodia.

Revolutionary Group coup; Sarit government.
Soviet Attache expelled for "activity dangerous to peace and security of nation."
Books of Communist Chinese origin found on sale in North-East, including one on techniques for coup d'etat.

INTERIM CONSTITUTION

1959 January: Ban on trade with China. February: Constituent Assembly; Sarit Prime Minister.
April: Board of Investment. July: ban on opium smoking. National Economic Development Corporation.
Government further restricted entry of Chinese to curb Communist infiltration, May 26.
Thailand-North Vietnam agreement signed August 14 for repatriation of 50,000 Vietnamese refugees in Thailand.
Supachai Srisati, Communist leader, executed July 6.

1960 Communist-inspired "Lawyers Group" distributed subversive leaflets in North-East, October.
NCNA publicized CPT Central Committee appeal to Thai people to form "broad patriotic front" against US and Thai Government.

1961 March: US 'East-West Highway'. May-July and December: North-East conspirators arrested.
October: Six Year Economic Plan starts. November: Second dispute with Cambodia.
Kularb Saipradit spoke over Peking Radio in Thai, January.
Thai Government in May publicly charged CPR and DRV with being instigators of plot to seize North-East Thailand.
Krong Chandavong, Communist leader in North-East Thailand, arrested and executed in May.
CPT document under title "Predictions for B.E. 2505 (1962)" distributed in Thailand calling for establishment of patriotic, democratic, united front, ousting of US "imperialist" and overthrow of Thai Government in terms of a "national liberation movement" in Thailand.

1962 Five Year Development Plan for the North-East.
March 6: US-Thai joint statement. May: US troops land in Thailand.
Ruam Wongphan, self-confessed Communist leader in Central Thailand, arrested in February and subsequently executed. Communist propaganda continues to hail him as a "patriot and hero."
CPT statutes published under false cover "junior Red Cross Manual" in 1961; seized February 23.

1963
"Voice of the People of Thailand," clandestine radio station operating from Yunnan Province (CPR), in Pathet Lao-held territory or from the DRV, began broadcasts beamed to Thailand in the Thai language, c. March 2. (By 1966 was broadcasting 28 hours per week.)
Second Thailand-North Vietnam agreement on Repatriation of Vietnamese refugees signed December 17.
Thanom-Prapass government (following Sarit's death).
"Movement for an Independent, Neutral and Nationalist Thailand" said by Communist media to have been established (reports of December). VPT communique, December 20, demanded that US withdraw from Thailand and that Thai Government adopt neutral policy.
"Voice of Movement for an Independent, Neutral and Nationalist Thailand" heard December 30.
(Neither the "Voice" nor the Movement has been heard from since).

From the early 1960s onward and with increasing American presence in Thailand, important dates in Thai history became more numerous and have been better recorded in the literature -- especially in the literature of the US Government. This list takes the reader through the difficult to find dates up through 1963.

Primary Sources: The work by Insor, the SEATO publication, and the RAC Histories listed in the bibliography.

FOOTNOTES

The security classification of material extracted from sources used in this report may be lower than the overall classification of the sources themselves, but it is no higher than the classification assigned to the corresponding paragraph of the text. The security classification of the content of this report was coordinated with, reviewed by, and approved by MACTHAI/JUSMAGTHAI and the US Embassy in Bangkok, the final approval authority of all US Government insurgency and counterinsurgency matters in Thailand. Also note that many pertinent documents are found on CHECO Secret Microfilm Rolls 875-878.

1. (S) Project CHECO Report Counterinsurgency in Thailand 1966 (U), 8 Nov 67;
   (S) Project CHECO Report COIN in Thailand January 1967-December 1968 (U), 26 Mar 69;
   (S) Project CHECO Report COIN in Thailand January 1969-December 1970 (U), 1 Jul 71.

2. (U) Thanom Kittikachorn, Prime Minister, RTG Communist Insurgency in Thailand, CSOC of the RTG, preface.

3. This paragraph and all of Chapter I are synthesized from the works listed in the Bibliography that describe the insurgency in Thailand. The prime sources used are as follows:

   (S) Dorothy K. Clark, M. Wanda Porterfield, and Roswell B. Wing, History of Insurgency/Counterinsurgency in Thailand (U), Research and Analysis Corporation (RAC), Jan 70 (Hereafter referred to as RAC History of I/CI);
   (THAI SECRET) Dorothy K. Clark, M. Wanda Porterfield, Roswell B. Wing, A History of Subversive Insurgency in Thailand Through 1967 (U), RAC, Jan 70 (Hereafter referred to as RAC History of I -- collectively, this and the RAC History of I/CI are hereafter referred to as RAC Histories);
   (S) Douglas S. Blaufarb, Organizing Counterinsurgency in Thailand, 1962-1970 (U), RAND, Aug 72 (Hereafter referred to as Blaufarb);
   (U) Royal Thai Government's (RTG) Communist Suppression Operations Command (CSOC), Communist Insurgency in Thailand, 1972 (Hereafter referred to as RTG White Paper);
   (C) Brief, J-2/USMACTHAI-JUSMAGTHAI, "Thailand Threat Brief, 6 Mar 72 (Hereafter referred to as "Threat Brief");
   (S/NF) Airgram, Department of State, US Embassy Bangkok Airgram A-355, Subj: Integrated Assessment of Security Assistance--Thailand FY1974-78 (U), Part II: Analysis of the Security Threats to Thailand, drafted 17 Aug 72 by F.B. Corry of the Political-Military Affairs (POMIL) Section (Hereafter referred to as "A-355").

The previously listed documents are hereafter collectively referred to as RAC Histories, et al.

4. (S)   RAC Histories, et al.;
   (S)   Critique of this report by Lt Col Max E. Newman, US Army, USMACTHAI/JUSMAGTHAI J-2.

5. (S)   RAC Histories, et al.;
   (U)   SEATO Short Paper No. 44, The Communist Threat to Thailand, Aug 67 (Hereafter referred to as SEATO publication).

6. (S)   RAC Histories, et al.;
   (U)   Discussion with Dr. James L. Woods of ARPA.

7. (S)   RAC Histories, et al.;
         Various atlases and geography books are the source for this section.
         The statistics on insurgents come from "Threat Brief" and the provincial insurgency locations from Lt Col Newman's critique.

8. (S)   RAC Histories, et al.;
   (C)   Brfgs by 13AF ADVON Directorate of Security Police.

9. Chapter II is mainly a synthesis of the material in the general works on Thailand some of which are listed in the Bibliography in Section One. Representative prime sources among these general works are as follows:

   (U)   Thomas F. Barton, Robert C. Kingsbury, and Gerald R. Showalter, Southeast Asia in Maps, Denoyer-Geppert, 1970 (Hereafter referred to as SEA in Maps);
   (U)   John E. Embree, Thailand-"A Loosely Structured Social System" in Loosely Structured Social Systems: Thailand in Comparative Perspective, Hans Dieter, Ed., Yale, 1969 (Hereafter referred to as "Embree");
   (U)   Charles A. Fisher, Southeast Asia, Dutton, 1964;
   (U)   D.G.E. Hall, A History of South-East Asia, 3rd ed., St Martin's 1968 (Hereafter referred to as Hall History);
   (U)   D.G.E. Hall, Ed., Atlas of Southeast Asia, St Martin's, 1964 (Hereafter referred to as Hall Atlas);
   (U)   D. Insor, Thailand: A Political, Social, and Economic Analysis, Praeger, 1963;
   (U)   Peter Kunstadter, Ed., Southeast Asian Tribes, Minorities, and Nations, Princeton, 1967.

10. (U) SEA in Maps;
    (U) Fisher;
    (U) Hall History;
    (U) Hall Atlas;

114

	(U)	Other general works. (General works are background sources for each paragraph of Chapter II. Only specific or additional sources are hereafter cited in Chapter II.)
11.	(S) (S) (S)	RAC Histories, et al.; Brfgs by 13th ADVON Directorate of Security Police; Brfgs by US Embassy/US Mission personnel in Thailand.
12.	(U) (S) (S)	Kunstadter; RAC Histories; Blaufarb.
13.	(S)	RAC Histories, et al.
14.	(U) (S)	Various Thai newspaper and general historical works contain examples of Thai besting foreigners in business dealings and upcountry Thai complaining about their treatment by Bangkok. RAC Histories, et al. (for example (S) Blaufarb, p. 6).
15.	(S)	RAC Histories, et al.
16.	(U)	Fisher, Insor, p. 175, and "Embree."
17.	(C)	Richard G. Sharp and Richard C. Rinkel, Revolution in a Non-Revolutionary Society, RAC, 1971.
18.	(U)	Attributed to the American Counsul, Chiang Mai, name unknown, per Mr. James L. Woods of ARPA.
19.	(U)	John Erros, Modeling the Economic Development of a Poorly Endowed Region: The Northeast of Thailand, RAND, 1970.
20.	(S)	RAC Histories, et al. and the general works on organizing counterinsurgency in Thailand.
21.	(S)	RAC Histories, et al. (for example Blaufarb, pp 3 and 7 and "A-355" pp 6-14. Chapter III is generally a synthesis of the background works on I/CI in Thailand which focus on individual and group involvement in the Thai insurgency. These works are listed in the bibliography and collectively are the source for each paragraph of Chapter III. Specific informational sources are noted only when required for clarity.
22.	(S)	RAC Histories, et al.
23.	(S) (S) (S/NF)	RAC Histories; Blaufarb; "A-355".

24. (S) RAC Histories;
    (S) Blaufarb;
    (C) Sharp and Rinkel.

25. (S) Ibid.

26. (C) Sharp and Rinkel is the prime source for the remainder of Chapter III.

27. (C) US Embassy, Bangkok, "General Concept for US Support of Thai Counterinsurgency," Tab J, 5 March 1973.

28. (S) RAC Histories; Blaufarb; "A-355"; and SEATO Publication are the prime sources for this paragraph and all of Chapter IV. Only additional sources are noted on subsequent paragraphs of Chapter IV, except where clarity requires repeating one or more of the basic sources.

29. (S) Blaufarb;
    (S) Lt Col Newman's critique.

30. (U) RTG/CSOC, Communist Prevention and Suppression Manual, Vol One: Concepts and Planning of Border Counter-Infiltration -- For Commanders and Staffs, June 1972 (Hereafter referred to as Border Manual);
    (C) Sharp and Rinkel.

31. (S) RAC History of I/CI, Chapters 10 and 12;
    (S) Blaufarb, Chapter III.

32. (S) RAC History of I/CI;
    (S) Blaufarb.

33. (S) Blaufarb, Chapter VI;
    (S) RAC History of I/CI, Part IV.

34. (S) Ibid.

35. (S) Ibid.

36. (S) Ibid.

37. (S) Ibid.

38. (U) Border Manual;
    (S) RAC History of I/CI, Part V and Summary;
    (S) Blaufarb, Summary and pp 126-128.

39. (S) Ibid.

40. (S) Ibid.

41. (S) Lt Col Newman's critique

42. (U) Conversations with Professor Shaumon McCune, Ph.D., Head of the Department of Geography, University of Florida, an American expert on East and Southeast Asia. Dr. McCune was associated with the China fund reallocations.

43. (U) Chapter V is a synthesis of the works about US assistance to Thai CI. These works are the sources for each paragraph of Chapter V. Where the information came primarily from one source it is noted. The main sources are (S) <u>RAC History of I/CI</u>, (S) <u>Blaufarb</u>, and RAC Field Office-Thailand, <u>US and International Organizations and Assistance Programs</u>, RAC, Dec 1969 (This report is Volume 7 in a series of reports, titled <u>Counterinsurgency Organizations and Programs in Northeast Thailand</u> prepared by RAC for ARPA and MRDC and hereafter referred to as <u>RAC Assistance</u>.)

44. (C) <u>RAC Assistance</u>, pp 1-7.

45. (S) <u>Blaufarb</u>, Chapters IV and V.

46. (S) <u>Blaufarb</u>, pp 43 and 53 (for SA/CI organization) and pp 61-62 for difficulties between Ambassador Martin and General Richard Stilwell, COMUSMACTHAI.

47. (C) US Embassy, Bangkok, "General Concept for US Support of Thai Counterinsurgency," 5 March 1973 (Hereafter referred to as "Concept");
    (C) US Embassy, Bangkok, "Guidelines" (for US support of Thai CI), Office of the SA/CI, ca. 1968.

48. (C) <u>RAC Assistance</u>.

49. (U) <u>Ibid</u>., pp 61-63.

50. (S) Brfgs by 13th AF ADVON Directorate of Security Police and US Embassy personnel.

51. (C) "Concept";
    (S) Brfgs by 13th AF ADVON Directorate of Security Police.

52. (C) "Concept."

53. (C) <u>RAC Assistance</u>.

54. (S) RAC Histories;
    (S) <u>Blaufarb</u>;
    (C) <u>RAC Assistance</u>.

55. (S)   Ibid.

56. (S)   Ibid.

57. (S)   RAC Histories;
    (S)   Blaufarb;
    (S)   Critique of this report by the US Embassy, Bangkok.

58. (S)   RAC Histories;
    (S)   Blaufarb;
    (C)   RAC Assistance

59. (C)   RAC Assistance.

60. (S)   RAC History of I/CI, Chapter 21;
    (S)   Blaufarb, p 100.

61. (S)   Blaufarb, pp 60-70.

62. (C)   Conversation with Mr. James L. Woods of ARPA.

63. (U)   Bangkok Post, Bangkok, Thailand, 4-6 January 1974.

BIBLIOGRAPHY

SECTION ONE: SELECTED GENERAL BACKGROUND WORKS

Barton, Thomas F.; Kingsbury, Robert C.; and Showalter, Gerald R. South east Asia in Maps. Chicago: Denoyer-Geppert, 1970. An excellent capsule overview of Southeast Asian History.

Benda, Harry J.; Larkin, John A.; and Mayer, Sydney L., Jr. The World of Southeast Asia-Selected Historical Readings. New York: Harper and Row, 1967. Entertaining and informative historical color.

Blanchard, Wendell. Thailand: its People, its Society, its Culture. New Haven: Human Relations Area Files, Inc. (HARF) Press, 1966. An authoritative cultural source book.

Buchanan, Keith. The Southeast Asian World-An Introductory Essay. Garden City, New York: Doubleday and Company, 1968.

Cady, John F. Southeast Asia-Its Historical Development. New York: McGraw-Hill, 1964. A standard, informative history.

Cady, John F. Thailand, Burma, Laos, and Cambodia. Englewood Cliffs, New Jersey: Prentice-Hall, 1966. A standard, informative history.

Coedès, G. The Making of South East Asia. Berkeley: University of California Press, 1966. Translated from French by H.M. Wright. A classic history.

Embree, John F. "Thailand-A Loosely Structured Social System," in Loosely Structured Social Systems: Thailand in Comparative Perspective. Hans Dieter, Editor. Yale University Southeast Asia Studies, Cultural Report Series No. 17. New Haven: Yale University, 1969. Describes Thai family and other social interactions. An excellent starting point for those unfamiliar with east Asian social systems.

Emos, John. Modeling the Economic Development of A Poorly Endowed Region: The Northeast of Thailand. Santa Monica, California: RAND (RM-6185-ARPA, ARPA Order No. 189-1), January 1970. Excellent regional development analysis.

Fisher, Charles A. South-East Asia-A Social, Economic and Political Geography. New York: Dutton, 1964. A classic geographic analysis of Southeast Asia. If one book could describe Southeast Asia, this is probably the one.

Fryer, Donald W. Emerging Southeast Asia-A Study in Growth and Stagnation. New York: McGraw-Hill, 1970. Excellent analysis of the economic geography of Southeast Asia.

Gurtov, Melvin. *Southeast Asian Relations with Communist China: Thailand, Cambodia, and Burma.* Santa Monica, California: RAND, June 1970. Considers spectrums of China's relations with Southeast Asia in areas of Peking's policies and policy instruments, with respect both to state-to-state relations and to revolutionary movements nearby. Deals with the place of China in the foreign and domestic policies of Thailand, Cambodia, and Burma. Correlates Chinese statements and actions with regard to elucidating its flexibility and spontaneity in addition to its ideological content. Analyzes the importance of China's impact on Southeast Asia. SECRET NOFORN

Hall, D.G.E. *A History of South-East Asia, 3rd Edition.* New York: St Martin's Press, 1968. One of the, if not *the* most authoritative histories of Southeast Asia.

Hall, D.G.E. *Atlas of Southeast Asia.* New York: St Martin's Press, 1964. Good regional atlas.

Herrmann, Albert. *An Historical Atlas of China.* Chicago: Aldine Publishing Company, 1966.

Insor, D. *Thailand: A Political, Social, and Economic Analysis.* New York: Praeger, 1963. Probably the most authoritative general analysis of the Thai sociological systems.

Kunstadter, Peter-Edition. *Southeast Asian Tribes, Minorities, and Nations.* Princeton, New Jersey: Princeton University Press, 1967. Two (2) volumes. Comprehensive ethnological survey.

Muscat, Robert J. *Development Strategy in Thailand.* New York: Praeger (Praeger Special Studies in International Economics and Development), 1966.

Pendleton, Robert L. *Thailand-Aspects of Landscape and Life.* New York: Duell, Sloan, and Pearce - An American Geographical Society Handbook, 1962. A classic geography of Thailand.

Perera, Walter - Editor. *Thailand Yearbook, 1966-1967.* Bangkok: Temple Publicity Services, 1966. Statistical source book.

Poole, Peter A. *The Vietnamese in Thailand: A Historical Perspective.* Ithaca, New York: Cornell University Press, 1970. Brief but comprehensive coverage of the Vietnamese minority in Thailand.

Riggs, Fred W. Thailand: *The Modernization of a Bureaucratic Policy.* Honolulu: East-West Center Press, 1966.

Rawson, R.R. *The Monsoon Lands of Asia.* Chicago: Aldine, 1963.

Robinson, Harry. *Monsoon Asia: A Geographical Survey.* New York: Praeger, 1967.

Seidenfaden, Erik. *The Thai Peoples*. Bangkok: The Siam Society, 1967.

Siffin, William J. *The Thai Bureaucracy*. Honolulu: East-West Center Press, 1966.

Skinner, G. William. *Chinese Society in Thailand: An Analytical History*. Ithica, New York: Cornell University Press, 1957.

Smith, Harvey H., et al. *Area Handbook for Thailand*. Washington: Department of the Army, 1968. Exceedingly comprehensive survey of Thailand.

Smith, Ronald Bishop. *Siam or The History of the Thais from Earliest Times to 1569AD.* Bethesda, Maryland: Decatur Press, 1966. One of the few histories covering the early Thai periods.

Spencer, J.E. and Thomas, William L. *Asia, East by South: A Cultural Geography, 2nd Edition*. New York: Wiley, 1971. A classic cultural geography of Southeast Asia.

Steinberg, David Joel - Editor. *In Search of Southeast Asia*. New York: Praeger, 1971.

Syamananda, Rong. *A History of Thailand*. Bangkok: Chulalongkorn University, January 1971. Thai history through the eyes of a Thai scholar.

Thompson, Virginia. *Thailand: The New Siam, 2nd Edition*. New York: Paragon Book Reprint Corporation, 1967. Unabridged reprint of the First Edition (1941), Secretariat, Institute of Pacific Relations, International Research Service. A classic history of Thailand.

SECTION TWO: GENERAL WORKS ON INSURGENCY AND COUNTERINSURGENCY IN THAILAND

Blaufarb, Douglas S. Organizing Counterinsurgency in Thailand. Santa Monica, California: RAND (ARPA: 189-1, R-1048-ARPA), August 1972. Only comprehensive report on this topic beyond 1967. SECRET

Battelle Memorial Institute/RACI. Advanced Research Projects Agency, Project AGILE, Semi-annual Report 2, 1 January-30 June 1964. October 1964. Reports on tasks according to sub-project areas: weapons, individual equipment, and rations: remote area mobility and logistics systems; communication systems; combat surveillance and target acquisition systems; individual and special projects; technical planning and programming; and research and exploratory development. CONFIDENTIAL

Battelle Memorial Institute/RACIC. Advanced Research Projects Agency, Project AGILE, Semi-annual Report No. 4, 1 January-30 June 1965. August 1965. Notes that program emphasis has shifted from development of "hardware" to studies in behavioral sciences, operations analysis, and systems integration. Reports on tasks according to sub-project areas: counterinsurgency analysis and requirements; environmental research; operations analysis in Vietnam, Thailand, Latin America, and the Middle East; information centers; weapons and surveillance projects; mobility, communications, and biomedical projects; and counterinsurgency systems integration. CONFIDENTIAL

Battelle Memorial Institute/RACIC. Advanced Research Projects Agency, Project AGILE, Semi-annual Report No. 5, 1 July-31 December 1965. February 1966. Discusses the status of research into weapons, surveillance, mobility, transportation, communications, biomedicine, nonlethal warfare, defoliation, environments, ecology, vegetation, and behavioral research. Reports on the status of the analysis of operations in Vietnam, Thailand, Latin America, the Middle East, and Africa. Discusses the mission and organization of ARPA/AGILE and comments on status of RACIC and CINFAC. CONFIDENTIAL

Battelle Memorial Institute/RACIC. Advanced Research Projects Agency, Project AGILE, Semi-annual Report No. 6, 1 January-30 June 1966. August 1966. Discusses the status of research into weapons, surveillance, mobility, transportation, communications, biomedicine, nonlethal warfare, defoliation, environments, ecology, vegetation, and behavioral research. Reports on the status of RACIC and the status of the analysis of operations in Vietnam, Thailand, Latin America, the Middle East, and Africa. Discusses the mission and organization of ARPA/AGILE. CONFIDENTIAL

Lucci, York. Final Report on Counterinsurgency Research and Analysis in Thailand. Palo Alto, California: Stanford Research Institute. September 1969. Summarizes research activities over a five-year period on insurgency in Southern Thailand; border control on Northeast Thailand; CI surveillance systems; and counterinsurgency communications. Covers investigation of the Communist Terrorist Organization, the Mekong River Surveillance System, and devices for detecting insurgency. CONFIDENTIAL

Morell, David L. The Implications of Thai Bureaucratic Policy for U.S. Assistance Strategy. Washington: National Security Council; AID, November 1969. Analyzes Thai bureaucratic policy and summarizes basic features of the Thai decision-making process. Identifies major factions and groups and principal interests and objectives of Thai leaders. Examines the importance of personal relationships to decision making and compares this to the role of institutional rivalry. Evaluates recent trends in bureaucratic power and influence. Discusses the US role as a catalyst and innovator of new programs and suggests alternate scenarios for Thai political change. Studies differences in Thai and US priorities and objectives, and problems of Thai political stability in the 1970s. Recommends changes in US advisory and training inputs to bring the programs into closer accord with Thai political realities. SECRET NOFORN.

Wing, Roswell B.; Clark, Dorothy K.; and Porterfield, M. Wanda. A History of Insurgency/Counterinsurgency in Thailand. Two volumes. Bangkok: RAC Field Office Thailand, January 1970. The authoritative compendium on the history of Thai Insurgency and Counterinsurgency through 1967. SECRET NOFORN

Wing, Roswell B.; Clark, Dorothy K.; and Porterfield, M. Wanda. A History of Subversive Insurgency in Thailand Through 1967. Bangkok: RAC Field Paper 26 029.202 (ARPA), Jan 70. THAI SECRET

Royal Thai Government, Communist Suppression Operations Command. Communist Prevention and Suppression Manual (English translation)
    Volume One - Concepts and Planning of Border Counter-Infiltration
              For Commanders and Staffs. June 1972.
    Volume Two (POI) - Village Information and Strike Force Courses, 1972.
    Volume Three - Villagers Handbook, 1972.
    Volume Four - Strike Force Handbook, 1972.
    (Volumes 2, 3, and 4 are bound together.)
    Bangkok: The Royal Thai Government, 1972.

Royal Thai Government, Communist Suppression Operations Command. Communist Insurgency in Thailand, A White Paper On. Bangkok: The Royal Thai Government, 1972.

RSSPIC, The Communist Threat to Thailand. RSSPIC, August 1967. The aim of this paper is to set forth the facts concerning the manner in which the continuing efforts to subvert and terrorize the Thai people and to undermine the stability and progressive development of Thai society are inspired, initiated, directed, and supported from outside the country. FOR OFFICIAL USE ONLY

Tanham, George K. (Book on Thailand)-(In Press). Holds promise of being an authoritative work on Thailand, its insurgency and counterinsurgency, through the eyes of a US Embassy official with first-hand knowledge of the situation from 1968 to 1970.

United States Government, Department of the Army, USARSUPTHAI. History of Communism in Thailand. Bangkok: US Govt, Dept of Army, USARSUPTHAI, November 1967. SECRET

United States Government, Department of the Army, USARPAC/G2, Insurgency Study, Thailand, Special Report 501. This study is an in-depth and comprehensive examination of the organization, techniques, tactics, and activities of the Communist Party of Thailand, the subversive support organization and the guerrillas. It provides a theoretical framework within which the insurgency in Thailand can be measured and understood. It is an analysis of Communist capabilities and courses of action in Thailand. The study is organized and written in a manner to be useful as a reference for intelligence analysts and planners and as a general orientation document on Thai insurgency. SECRET

Wasilewski, Thomas et al. Scenario of Advanced Phase I insurgency in Thailand. August 1967. SECRET NOFORN

SECTION THREE: SELECTED LISTING OF MORE NARROWLY FOCUSED WORKS ON COUNTER-INSURGENCY IN THAILAND AND RELATED TOPICS. (Nearly all of these works were initiated by the US Advanced Research Projects Agency (ARPA) (DOD) or associated in some way with ARPA.)

Advanced Research Projects Agency (ARPA). Test Plan for Mekong River Border Control Subsystem. March 1967. Describes test data inputs needed for designing a system for improving the Laos-Thailand border control program. Explains the test plan in terms of design, management, evaluation, support training, monitoring, and data collection. Covers Thai and US support needed, operating role arrangements, and scheduling. Deals with test design parameters, equipment and personnel required, and reporting procedures. Contains MRS field test support contract work statement. CONFIDENTIAL

ARPA. Summary Report Royal Thai Navy Sattaship Region Security System Development Program (Draft). June 1971. CONFIDENTIAL

American Institute for Research/Center for Research in Social Systems (AIR/CRSS). Characteristics of Selected Societies Relevant to U.S. Military Interests: Thailand Volume III (U). August 1970. SECRET NOFORN

AIR. A Preliminary Evaluation of: The Village Police Program in Udorn Sakon Nakhon, and Kalasin. January 1970. UNCLASSIFIED

Battelle Memorial Institute. An Annotated Bibliography with Additional Comments on the RTG Defector Program. January 1971. SECRET NOFORN

Battelle Memorial Institute. Royal Thai Government Interaction with the Non-Thai Ethnic Minorities in the North: A Program Review and Recommendations for US Mission Support. Task No A-3660. November 1971. CONFIDENTIAL

Booz-Allen Applied Research Inc. A Village Alarm for Thailand, Phase II. November 1968. Explains need for Village Alarm System (VAS) for village protection and its importance to the RTG. Describes system parameters for VAS in Changwad Nakhon Phanom, basic radio element, radio evaluation, and compares cost of provincial system, USOM FM series vs. Citizens Band (CB) equipment. Considers power source problems, assembly and testing of VAS radios, conversion to alarm configurations and muban installation. Lists basic equipment needed for tamboon VAS readout terminal. Cost estimates are presented. CONFIDENTIAL

Booz-Allen Applied Research Inc. A Village Alarm System for Thailand, Technical Report on Phase I (U)-Field Draft-Volume I. November 1968. Defines problem of Communist Terrorist harrassment of villages and points out desirability of an alarm system that could be employed by pressured villages. Gives background of village alarm system (VAS) and notes its employment in Kenya, Malaya, and South Vietnam. Describes the ARPA/USOM

Hamlet Alarm System established in Vietnam in 1962. Outlines operational requirements of establishing a VAS at the mubon-tambol level. Discusses Royal Thai Government programs and US Mission programs pertinent to a VAS. Describes types of systems and 3 basic configurations of VAS. Discusses development of VAS technical requirements, the effects of physical environment upon requirements and design of a village alarm system. Describes a proposed concept village alarm system in Nakhon Phanom; gives cost analysis and provides a test plan for equipment suitability. CONFIDENTIAL

Booz-Allen Applied Research, Inc. A Village Alarm System for Thailand Report on Phase I (U)-Field Draft-Volume II. November 1968. Summarizes problem of village harassment, and the examination of the operational, technical and environmental requirements for an alarm system at the muban-tambol level. Appendix A describes the physical and cultural geography of changwad Nakhon Phanom covering location, border, Nakhon Phanom Lowlands, the "Phu Phan Region," drainage, soils, vegetation, weather and climate. Discussion of cultural geography includes: administrative data of 8 amphoes and 2 king amphoes, transportation, communication, electric power, and agriculture. Appendix B contains reference tables, for VHF Radio wave propagation to be used in conjunction with technical specifications presented in Volume I. Appendix C contains a series of interviews reports conducted in support of the Requirements Task of the VAS. Appendix D reports an examination of radio and alarm equipment suitability for VAS in Thailand. CONFIDENTIAL

Booz-Allen Applied Research, Inc. A Village Alarm System for Thailand Technical Report on Phase II(U)-Field Draft-Volume I Communications Equipment Requirements. December 1968. Reports on the initial technical implementation of Concept Village Alarm System (VAS). Discusses developments in equipment requirements for the Concept VAS. Diagrams show implementation step of Concept I with additional equipment. Outlines the communications engineering requirements for the overt muban alarm transceiver. Gives simplified schematic diagram and basic technical specifications for FM-1 and FM-5 radios. Discusses conversion of basic radio to village alarm muban station, the Sandia Hamlet Alarm System and the ARPA-USOM Village Alarm System. Points out problems and makes recommendations regarding operational problems in the implementation of Concept 2. CONFIDENTIAL

Booz-Allen Applied Research, Inc. A Village Alarm System for Thailand Technical Report on Phase II (U)-Volume II, Selection of Transceivers for the Basic Radio Element. January 1969. Presents background on a Concept Village Alarm System and methodology used in the study. Reports on technical aspects of the suitability of the OPS/FM-1A and the OPS/FM-5A for the transceiver element of Village Alarm System (VAS). Suggests alternative transceivers for VAS. Discusses effects of the physical and operational environment on the selection of a transceiver. Examines feasibility of establishing a Very High Frequency VAS net between muban and tambol. Compares basic cost tradeoffs between OPS/FM-1A and OPS/FM-5A and transceivers operating in the Citizen's Band. CONFIDENTIAL

Cornell Aeronautical Laboratory. <u>Preliminary System Definition for Village Security System, Final Report Task 4</u>. May 1964. Defines the elements required to achieve village security. Uses Nakhon Phanom as a model to study for relationships between CT incidents, security force strength, and security force cost. Examines various methods and equipment used in security system as they apply to environment, CT location and strength, and reaction capability. Contains statistical and cost data. CONFIDENTIAL

Cornell Aeronautical Laboratory. <u>Preliminary System Studies Supporting Village Security Analysis (U) Task 4 (Subtask A)</u>. May 1968. Provides inputs to a follow-on, in-depth village security systems study, which will culminate in recommendations for village security systems. Describes the environment of a village security system and the process by which characteristics of an "average" village in certain amphoes were derived. Discusses Communist threat to villages. Develops the elements of a security system; defines and analyzes factors to be considered in a model of village security system; and analyzes a reaction capability. Considers an approach to village security of an interface between security related development and military or police force. Provides an analysis of the relationships among security force costs, security force and CT incidents in Nakhon Phanom. CONFIDENTIAL

Cornell Aeronautical Laboratory. <u>Project AMPIRT ARPA Multiband Photographic and Infrared Reconnaissance Test, Final Report, Volume VI</u>. Studies ways to improve daytime aerial photo-reconnaissance in terms of procedural and technological changes. Evaluates the elements of photo collection, processing and interpretation. Reports on test flight missions over Vietnam and Thailand in search of insurgent activity in delta and forested terrain, to map supplement photographic missions, and to search for permanent type enemy installations. CONFIDENTIAL

Institute for Defense Analyses (IDA), Weapons Systems Evaluation Group. <u>Counterinsurgency in Thailand (U) Volume I: Summary and Evaluation</u>. June 1968. Describes Thailand's international position, geography and people, economy and political administration of central and local government. Summarizes history of Communist Party of Thailand (CPT) and developing insurgency in all regions of Thailand. Describes the insurgent threat and tactics employed by insurgents to establish an infrastructure and gain support of Thai villagers. Evaluates the economic and political capabilities to cope with the insurgency, and concepts and organization for counterinsurgency. Discusses environmental improvement, police and paramilitary forces, and Royal Thai Armed Forces. Theorizes on the growth potential for the insurgency, capability of RTG to cope with the threat, and the implications for US support. SECRET

IDA, Wps Sys Eval Gp. <u>Counterinsurgency in Thailand (U) Volume II: Political, Economic, and Social Background</u>. June 1968. Examines political factors that affect the ability of the Thais to cope with the insurgency in their country. Focuses on attitudes towards RTG of ethnic Thai majority,

Sino-Thai, Thai-Lao, Thai-Malay, and hill tribes. Discusses the influence of the Buddhist Church and the political parties. Describes the roles of the monarchy, the military leadership and the civil service, and the national policy of political liberalization and alignment with USA. Outlines local administration. Analyzes the Thai economy and prospects for national economic development to include the economic capability of RTG to support its counterinsurgency effort. Examines prospects of Thai Communists for establishing a Thai peasant base for a mass insurgency, describes preconditions to insurgency, forces for change, incompatibility of Communist and Thai values, susceptibility of Thai peasant youth, and Communist tactics in N.E. Thailand. SECRET

IDA, Wpns Sys Eval Gp. Counterinsurgency in Thailand (U) Volume III: Historical Analyses of Other Counterinsurgencies. June 1968. Discusses principles of counterinsurgency derived from literature and study of other insurgencies regarding response to insurgency, support for and from the population, and intelligence and counterintelligence requirements. Analyzes military strategy and tactics in low-level counterinsurgency operations, emphasizing missions and task of armed forces and paramilitary forces. Discusses offensive strategy constraints and territorial organization of military forces. Proposes principles for tailoring infantry battalions and operations for fragmentation and attrition of guerrillas. SECRET

IDA, Wpns Sys Eval Gp. Environmental Improvement, from Counterinsurgency in Thailand (U) Volume IV: Appendixes: The Insurgent Threat and the RTG Counterinsurgency Effort. June 1968. Describes the nature and emphasis of the principal environmental improvement programs of the RTG counterinsurgency effort. Examines objectives, organization, and financial support of the programs. Covers Accelerated Rural Development (ARD), noting roadbuilding, water control and storage, training equipment operators and technicians, Mobile Medical Teams, Amphur Farmer Groups, and Agricultural Package Program. Reports on Mobile Development Units; the programs of the Ministry of Interior: Community Development, Developing Democracy, and Remote Area Security Development; of the Ministries of Public Health, Education, National Development, and Defense. Discusses economic, social, and political results of these programs. Discusses the Northeast Economic Development Plan (NEED). SECRET

IDA, Wpns Sys Eval Gp. The Insurgent Threat from Counterinsurgency in Thailand (U) Volume IV: Appendixes: The Insurgent Treat and the RTG Counterinsurgency Effort. June 1968. Presents chronology of the insurgency in Thailand and describes the Communist Party (CPT) organization. Discusses the CPT strategy for revolution, techniques of persuasion and coercion, and training. Describes problems of the regional movements in leadership, friction between Sino-Thais and ethnic Thais, underdeveloped command structure, and failure to generate popular support. SECRET

IDA, Wpns Sys Eval Gp. <u>Intelligence Capability, from Counterinsurgency in Thailand (U) Volume IV: Appendixes: The Insurgent Threat and the RTG Counterinsurgency Effort</u>. June 1968. Evaluates the performance of the RTG in developing an intelligence organization capable of identifying the membership of the insurgent infrastructure and furnishing paramilitary and military forces with intelligence. Traces the evolution of the intelligence capability from the out-break of insurgency in 1962. Describes responsibilities and operations of special Branch, National Police, and Joint Security Centers. Outlines the current intelligence structure. SECRET

IDA, Wpns Sys Eval Gp. <u>Police, Village Security, and Paramilitary Programs, from Counterinsurgency in Thailand (U) Volume IV: Appendixes: The Insurgent Threat and the RTG Counterinsurgency Effort</u>. June 1968. Outlines organization of Thai National Police Department (TNPD), the Metropolitan Police, Education Bureau, Provincial Police Division, Border Patrol Police, Central Investigation Bureau, and Police Air Division. Discusses police image and police activities in the Northeast, covering patrols, sweep operations, response operations, intelligence collection, population and resources control, and psychological operations. Describes village security units: Volunteer Defense Corps, Volunteer Protection Teams, Peoples Assistance Teams, Village Security Officers, and Village Security Forces. Discusses Border Patrol Police, Provincial Police Special Action Forces, and the Volunteer Defense Corps. SECRET

IDA, Wpns Sys Eval Gp. <u>Royal Thai Armed Forces, from Counterinsurgency in Thailand (U) Volume IV: Appendixes: The Insurgent Threat and the RTG Counterinsurgency Effort</u>. June 1968. Provides data for an evaluation of the capabilities and limitations of the Royal Thai Armed Forces to counter insurgency. Outlines suppression operations in Northeast Thailand, and North Thailand. Presents organization and procurement, manpower resources and personnel constraints. Covers equipment, training, and logistics of RTA. Summarizes mission, capabilities and limitations, and inventories of Royal Thai Air Force and Royal Thai Navy. SECRET

Lockheed Missiles and Space Company. <u>Airbase Defense Systems Study-Thailand, Final Technical Report (U)</u>. Aug 1970. CONFIDENTIAL

Military Research and Development Center (MRDC). <u>Evaluation and Engineering Test of the Westland SRN-5 Hovercraft in Thailand</u>. Apr 1966. FOR OFFICIAL USE ONLY

MRDC. <u>Evaluation and Engineering Test of the Shallow Draft Boat in Thailand</u>. May 1966. UNCLASSIFIED

MRDC. <u>Vehicle Characteristics Affecting Mobility in Thailand</u>. May 1966. UNCLASSIFIED

MRDC. Directory of Potential Highway Airstrips in Thailand (Vol 1 - NE Thailand. July 1966. UNCLASSIFIED

MRDC. Individual Cooking Equipment for the Royal Thai Armed and Paramilitary Forces. July 1968. UNCLASSIFIED

MRDC. Royal Thai Armed Forces Vehicles Equipment with Terra Tires. November 1968. UNCLASSIFIED

MRDC. Meo Handbook. October 1969. UNCLASSIFIED

MRDC. Study of Youth in Northeast Thailand (U). January 1970. FOR OFFICIAL USE ONLY

MRDC. Environmental Data Atlas for East Thailand. September 1970. UNCLASSIFIED

MRDC. Evaluation of the Effectiveness of Selected Village Security Units in Three Changwats in Northeast Thailand. (English Language Version) September 1970. CONFIDENTIAL

MRDC. Problems Associated with Rural Land Tenure in Thailand. October 1970. UNCLASSIFIED

MRDC. Airbase Defense Thailand-Report on Airbase Defense Systems at Udorn RTAFB. January 1971. CONFIDENTIAL

MRDC. Village Leadership in Northeast Thailand. (The Case of Nakhon Phanom) February 1971. UNCLASSIFIED

MRDC. Handbook, Insurgency Defense and Suppression (Communist Defense and Suppression Division) Vol I. (Thai Version) CONFIDENTIAL

MRDC. Directory of Tribal Villages in Northern Administrative Divisions-Changwat Chiang Mai (13). April 1971. UNCLASSIFIED

RAND Corporation (RAND). Certain Effects of Culture and Social Organization of Internal Security in Thailand (U). September 1963. Discusses awareness of the Communist threat in Thai villages, Communist radio broadcasts, and the problem of Thai village administration. Villagers' attitudes toward government are considered, as well as official corruption, the structure of authority and flow of information. Presents suggestions for an administration. CONFIDENTIAL

RAND. Thailand Airfields and Airstrips: A Compilation of Physical Climatic and Facility Data (U) Volume I. March 1967. This is the first volume of a two-volume Memorandum concerned with compilation and analysis of data on airfields and airstrips in Thailand. Physical characteristics, facilities, logistic support, potential and planned future construction are major categories used in the compilation. SECRET

RAND. Thailand Airfields and Airstrips: An Analysis of Physical, Climatic and Facility Data (U) Volume II. March 1967. This report analyzes data concerning airfields and airstrips in Thailand. Emphasis is laid on those facilities that are considered important to a general picture of airfield utilization for studies of mobility, trafficability, and logistics. The analysis also provides data useful for aircraft configuration studies and parametric studies of military air systems. Maps show the geographic distribution of 164 land plans (and two seaplane) facilities. These are identified, classified as primary, secondary, tertiary and other airfields, and their useability status is given. Temperature, rainfall, and elevation statistics are given as are runway lengths and weightbearing capabilities. SECRET

RAND. Seminar on Development and Security in Thailand: Part I, The Insurgency. March 1969. Outlines principal problem areas: development-security interrelationship; efficacy of the insurrectionary movement; relevance of programs; and urgent tasks for research. Focuses on the nature of the insurgency: what is known about CTs; recruitment appeals and "alternatives" offered by insurgents; and tactics used in exploiting Thai vulnerabilities. Discusses government information systems and the possible effect of development programs on insurgency. Examines most promising areas for research. Includes contributed papers "Communist Terrorist Operations in Northeast Thailand: Organizational and Psychological Aspects," by Richard Sharp, and "Relating Rebellion to the Environment: An Econometric Approach," by Edward J. Mitchell. (Part II is located in Accession Number 07856). CONFIDENTIAL

Research Analysis Corporation (RAC). Supply Requirements for Royal Thai Government Deployment in Advanced Insurgency in Northeast Thailand. December 1964. Estimates the supply requirements of the RTG counterinsurgent forces to be used for planning purposes in transportation problems. Gives requirements of specific forces and ratings. Statistics are based on capability to mount combat operations, mobility requirements, and probable rates of fire, data on food, vehicles, fuel, armor, aircraft, and ammunition are given. Contains statistical tables. CONFIDENTIAL

RAC. Border Patrol Police Capabilities and Potentials for Counterinsurgency in Thailand (U). April 1966. Discusses the potential insurgency problem of Thai border areas and functions of the Border Patrol Police. Refers to the threat along the Malaysian, Burma, Laotian, and Cambodian borders. Describes BPP organization, recruitment, equipment and training. Also reports on intelligence collection and transmission, civic action, and BPP relations with RTG organizations and officials. Contains appendices on platoon locations, subjects covered in training courses, and communications network. CONFIDENTIAL

RAC. Vulnerability of the Highway and Railway Systems in Northeast Thailand (U). October 1966. Assesses the vulnerability to insurgent interdiction of the surface lines of communication in NE Thailand as part of the system of logistical support for advanced-phase counterinsurgency operations;

determines vulnerable route segments; proposes measures to reduce line of communication vulnerability and minimize the effects of insurgent attack. Discusses vulnerability of bridges to sabotage. Contains maps and photographs. CONFIDENTIAL

RAC. Vulnerability of Thailand's Electric Power System to Insurgent Sabotage or Attack (U). October 1966. Assesses the vulnerability of Thailand's electric power system to insurgent sabotage or attack. All the major generation, transmission, and distribution systems and their existing security measures are described. CONFIDENTIAL

RAC. Analysis of the Mobile Reserve Platoon Program: An Element of Thailand's Border Patrol Police (DRAFT). March 1967. Documents and provides a preliminary analysis of a developing counterinsurgency activity--The Mobile Reserve Platoon (MRP) program of the Border Patrol Police (BPP)--from its inception through deployment and use of these units throughout Thailand. CONFIDENTIAL

RAC. Examples of Insurgent Propaganda Themes in Northeast and South Thailand. May 1967. This is an interim report on a continuing study of insurgent psychological operations in Thailand. It presents illustrations of persistent propaganda themes drawn from translations of insurgent written propaganda, and should be of interest to those concerned with the nature of the subversive threat in Thailand. CONFIDENTIAL

RAC. A Vulnerability Analysis of the Lines of Communications for RTG Counterinsurgency Operations in Northeast Thailand (U). September 1967. SECRET (Thai and US only)

RAC. Counterinsurgency Systems Manual Northeast Thailand (U) Phase 2 Report, Annex A, Special Strike Teams and Census Aspiration Cadres. 1968. This report analyzes the two subject organizations with respect to their background, mission, organization, funding, locations and strengths, personnel and training equipment, activities, interrelationships, and reporting schedules. SECRET

RAC. Insurgent Network Analysis: Northeast Thailand (U) RAC-TP-312. April 1968. The purpose of this report is to analyze the insurgency in Northeast Thailand by using selected analytic approaches in a program of research leading to the development of data-management systems and techniques for use in providing intelligence support to counterinsurgency military questions. SECRET

RAC. Insurgent Network Analysis: Northeast Thailand (U), Appendix E, Communist Infiltration Routes and Distribution Patterns in Thailand. May 1966. CONFIDENTIAL

RAC. Insurgent Network Analysis: Northeast Thailand (U), Appendix E, Communist Infiltration Routes and Distribution Patterns in Thailand (U). CONFIDENTIAL

RAC. _Incipient Safe Havens in Northeast Thailand (U)_. August 1968. SECRET

RAC. _Insurgent Base and Support Systems of Northeast Thailand, A Preliminary Model (U)_. September 1968. Reports on insurgent situation in the Phu Phan hills and organization of guerrilla units. Describes environmental components of guerrilla base: haven zone, support zone and contact zone. Discusses development of the base and support system, guerrilla base areas, and organization of Kan Luang CT group, and Nong Bo Group. Home-camp area, outpost camps, training and indoctrination sites and staging camps are described. Support system is considered in terms of village support group, and external support system. Appendix contains a map of analogue model of the CT base and support system of the Central Phu Phan Mts., and a table summarizing relevant intelligence data. CONFIDENTIAL

RAC. _Insurgent Operations in North Thailand, A Study of Insurgent Adaptiveness in Penetration of the Northern Hill Tribes_. November 1968. Discusses research focus, approach, effort and organization of results. Comments on pragmatism of insurgents. Describes phases of insurgent activity, covering involvement with the Pathet Lao, infiltration of initial cadre, exfiltration of native cadre, reinfiltration and spread of the movement, and overt acts of violence. Summarizes incident and casualty data and the current status of insurgent penetration. Contrasts the Northeast insurgent operations, noting cross border support, professionalization, and propensity for violence. Discusses characteristics of the Meo, their internal sociocultural vulnerabilities, and barriers and conflicts between Meo and other hill tribes. Analyzes Communist propaganda and recruitment in tribal villages, presenting examples of insurgent targeting of villages. Includes insurgent propaganda themes. CONFIDENTIAL

RAC. _Counterinsurgency Organizations & Programs in NE Thailand, Vol 1 (Command and Control Organization)_. December 1969. CONFIDENTIAL

RAC. _Counterinsurgency Organizations and Programs in Northeast Thailand, Vol 2 (Military Organizations and Programs)_. SECRET

RAC. _Counterinsurgency Organizations and Programs in NE Thailand, Vol 3 (Paramilitary Organizations and Programs)_. July 1968. CONFIDENTIAL

RAC. _Counterinsurgency Organizations and Programs in NE Thailand, Vol 4 (Police Organizations and Programs)_. December 1969. CONFIDENTIAL

RAC. _Counterinsurgency Organizations and Programs in NE Thailand, Vol 5 (Development Organizations and Programs)_. December 1969. UNCLASSIFIED

RAC. _Counterinsurgency Organizations and Programs in NE Thailand, Vol 6 (Health Improvement Organizations and Programs)_. UNCLASSIFIED

RAC. Counterinsurgency Organizations and Programs in NE Thailand, Vol 7 (US and International Organizations and Assistance Programs). December 1969. CONFIDENTIAL

RAC. Insurgent Organization and Operational Patterns: A Primer for Northeast Thailand. 1969. Deals with the Communist Party of Thailand (CPT) and insurgent organization within Thailand: insurgent operating patterns and their counterinsurgency implications; and the method of operation of insurgent cadre. Describes CPT structure from the village to the central command. Examines insurgent movements and recommends response. Describes functional roles within insurgent infrastructures.

RAC. Summaries of Eleven Interviews on Insurgent Psychological Operations in North Thailand. February 1969. Covers interviews with Border Patrol Police team leaders, Black Meo paramilitary personnel, a USOM contractor, Black Meo village leader and trader, member of PSYOPS staff, nai amphoes, JSC-5 personnel, and a Thai officer of Third Army Forward. Reports on length of time terrorists have been in the area, relationship across Lao border between Meo clans, CT supporters in the villages, fighting ability of the Meo, and Communist efforts in the area. Covers differences between RTG and hill tribes, training of guerrillas, effects of government propaganda on the hill tribes, and Communist recruitment patterns. CONFIDENTIAL

RAC. Insurgent Basing Counteroperations, Military Intelligence Aspects-in Northeast Thailand. April 1969. CONFIDENTIAL

RAC. Revolution in a Non-Revolutionary Society: An Exploratory Analysis of Insurgent-Villager Interactions in Thailand. July 1969. Extends a descriptive analysis of insurgent psychological operations and recruitment in Thailand conducted in 1967. Relates this analysis, in an exploratory manner, to relevant factors in Thai villager behavior, attitudes, and environment so as to develop a theoretical perspective on insurgent-villager interactional patterns. CONFIDENTIAL

RAC. Counterinsurgency Organizations and Programs in Northeast Thailand: Development Organizations and Programs, Vol 5. December 1969. Lists the RTG organizations engaged in counterinsurgency activities. Covers the Mobile Development Units, village-oriented development programs, Accelerated Rural Development, national infrastructure development programs, and agricultural development programs. UNCLASSIFIED

RAC. Police Organizations and Programs. December 1969. Gives an overview of police organizations and programs in Thailand. Discusses the air police, marine police, highway patrol police, railway police, and forestry police, with special emphasis on the activities of the Border Patrol Police and the Provincial Police in Northeastern Thailand. Comments on the strength, funding, logistical support, location, training, equipment, effectiveness, and US support in each of the police units. CONFIDENTIAL

RAC. Counterinsurgency Intelligence Applications for Operations in Northeast Thailand, A Course of Instruction, Vol I. January 1970. Presents a description of a proposed course of instruction on methods of collating the types of intelligence pertinent to insurgency in the Northeast. Covers collation and display of data needed to support the intelligence format modified for CI purposes proposed in "Insurgent Basing Counteroperations, Military Intelligence Aspects in Northeast Thailand," April 1969. Gives background information on insurgent organization and activities. Covers insurgent-related and friendly activity reporting, modified intelligence estimate for CI, intelligence data collation techniques, and map training exercise. (Related document is located in Accession Number 17077.) CONFIDENTIAL

RAC. Counterinsurgency Intelligence Applications for Operations in Northeast Thailand, A Course of Instruction, Vol II. January 1970. Consists of appendixes to Volume I. Contains outline of course of instruction, terminology for CPT organizational echelons, sample of written insurgent propaganda, and contact/CT activity report forms. Shows sample CSOC daily intelligence summaries, map symbol definitions, Ban Nong Phakthiem insurgent activity file, and civic action report form. Contains sample intelligence appreciation and psychological warfare plan for Malaya. Gives sample conventional military intelligence estimate, environmental data unit definitions, village information reporting forms, type indications of guerrilla warfare, and map exercise material. (Related document is located in Accession Number 17068.) CONFIDENTIAL

RAC. The Sources of Involvement, the Northeast Thai Villager and His Introduction into an Insurgent Movement (U). January 1970. CONFIDENTIAL

RAC. Counterinsurgency Intelligence Applications for Operations in Northeast Thailand; Summary of Approved Draft Technical Report DS-70-10. April 1970. Presents a proposed course of instruction on methods of collating the types of intelligence pertinent for operations during a Phase I insurgency such as that in Northeast Thailand. Gives source of material to be presented and duration of course. Outlines course coverage: Communist Party of Thailand organizations; insurgent-related and friendly-activity reporting; proposed modification of the Military Intelligence Estimate format; and collation techniques to support the modified format. Notes that an additional unit of instruction includes analyses of the environment, a system of village files, and the insurgent activity pattern. CONFIDENTIAL

RAC. Development and Security Organizations and Programs in North Thailand (U). May 1971. THAI SECRET

RAC. Revolution in a Non-Revolutionary Society (U), The Process of Involvement in Rural Insurgency in Thailand (U). June 1971. CONFIDENTIAL

Stanford Research Institute (SRI). <u>Materiel Used by Communist Terrorists in South Thailand</u>. January 1965. Contains lists of clothing, personal items, food, livestock, medicine, weapons, communications equipment, fuels, tools, construction supplies, containers, lamps, batteries, stationery and printing supplies, and recreation equipment used by Communist Terrorists in South Thailand. CONFIDENTIAL

SRI. <u>Eleven Communist Terrorist Camps in Southern Thailand.</u> February 1965. Describes and illustrates diagrammatically the physical layout of each camp, and estimates number of CTs who used camp. Appendix contains report to visit to Border Patrol Police 9th area headquarters near Songkhla by the author, describing CT camps visited. CONFIDENTIAL

SRI. <u>Descriptive Analysis of the Largest Communist Terrorist Camp Discovered in South Thailand.</u> March 1965. This report describes the events leading up to the discovery of the subject camp, gives a description of the camp and the area surrounding it, and lists the materiel discovered in the camp. The significance of the camp with respect to the size and organization of guerrilla forces in the area is discussed. CONFIDENTIAL

SRI. <u>Counterinsurgency Communications Requirements in Southeast Asia: Final Report</u>. June 1965. Explains methodology of research and structure of the report. Summarizes results of communications requirements as they are applicable to low-intensity and medium-intensity counterinsurgency. Discusses research and development implications of findings. Covers specialized design considerations related to Thai intelligibility and human factors. Contains a model for the evaluation of Border Patrol Police communication and a description of an alogic simulation of guerrilla revolution. Discusses quantification of terrain effect on line of sight. SECRET

SRI. <u>Counterinsurgency Communications Requirements in Southeast Asia: Final Report, Annex A.</u> June 1965. Deals with the environment of Thailand. Covers geography, meteorology, population, and education. Reports on transportation and communications facilities. Discusses government structure. Considers state of subversion and insurgency and potentially subversive groups. Describes counterinsurgent forces, covering the Ministry of Defense and the police system. SECRET

SRI. <u>Counterinsurgency Communications Requirements in Southeast Asia: Annex C.</u> June 1965. Covers requirements for small unit counterinsurgency combat operations in tropical areas. Reviews concepts, organization, and tactics of insurgency and counterinsurgency. Discusses small unit operations in terms of area organization, combat operations, and reconnaissance and combat patrols. Considers correlation of communications requirements for small units, covering tactical functions and command-control elements. Describes essential operational requirements: simplicity, traffic capacity, stability, ease of maintenance, and planned obsolescence. SECRET

SRI. *Aerial Photography, Mapping and Village Location*. March 1966. Discusses plans for development of the Northeast in order to counter the increasing insurgency. Explains how accurate maps are necessary for implementing development plans. Describes the types of maps being used throughout the US mission. Suggests an updating of these maps through aerial photographic coverage, noting how this coverage will enable places to be pinpointed through use of the Universal Transverse Mercator (UTM) Grid System. Outlines a plan for implementing aerial photographing of the Northeast. SECRET

SRI. *Low-Intensity Counterinsurgency: A Study of the Border Patrol Police of Thailand*. May 1966. Describes the organization, mission, operations, and communications of the Thai Border Patrol Police (BPP) as a basis for establishing communications systems requirements for low-intensity counterinsurgency. Discusses the operational procedures, facilities, installations and equipment, maintenance and maintenance problems, training methods, records, and traffic of the BPP communications systems. SECRET NOFORN

SRI. *Requirements for Counterinsurgency Surveillance in Southern Thailand: The Integrated Results of the SRI Surveillance Project, April 1964-March 1966 (U)*. October 1966. The first half of this report presents descriptive materials and preliminary analyses concerning the nature and detectability of various Communist Terrorist (CT) activities, notably those connected with logistics and the jungle camps in which many of the CTs live. The latter half draws together these materials in an analysis of the degrees and kinds of requirements for surveillance systems that might be used against the CTs in Southern Thailand. Three kinds of systems--rubidium vapor magnetometers, seismic detectors, and infrared scanners--are analyzed in depth; several others that were investigated more briefly during the two-year period receive lesser treatment. For each system, the requirements for procurement and use, equipment development, and/or operations analysis and field testing are estimated. CONFIDENTIAL

SRI. *Counterinsurgency Communications Requirements in Thailand (U)*. December 1966. Presents a final report of SRI's Southeast Asia Communications Research (SEACORE). Summarizes research tasks: examination of the communication systems and capabilities required to adequately support Thai strategies and operations for low-intensity and medium-intensity counterinsurgency activities; a survey of existing communications systems; an evaluation of the hindrance to oral Thai communication presented by certain design characteristics of voice communication equipment in use; and a survey of human engineering factors and aptitudes of Thai personnel. CONFIDENTIAL

SRI. *Insurgent Interrogations and Interviews, Northeast Thailand, Vol I*. 1967. Contains compendium of reports of interrogations of surrendered and captured insurgents obtained from Thai counterinsurgency officials operating within Northeast Thailand. Gives biography, area of capture or surrender, and a review of duties and experiences as a CT. Covers indoctrination; training; reasons for joining CTs; location of camps; arms, ammunitions and supplies. Includes detailed accounting of names and locations of associates and relatives. CONFIDENTIAL

SRI. <u>A Collection of Trip Reports and Interview Memoranda Used in Preparing Stanford Research Institute Research Memorandum 10.</u> March 1967. Consists of interviews held with government officials in Changwats Yala and Songkhla, and in government departments in Bangkok, dealing with questions of insurgency and counterinsurgency, population and resource controls. The problem of resettlement and village regrouping is dealt with. Problems of the rubber industry, mining, and forestry as they relate to counterinsurgency are discussed. Government corruption is reported. CONFIDENTIAL-NOFORN

SRI. <u>Interrogations of Surrendered Enemy Personnel.</u> July 1967. Contains translation of impromptu interrogation of SEPs assembled in Yala. Illustrates opportunities for applications of remote monitoring equipment deployed in the CT environment. Evaluates vulnerability of CT logistics system to detection. Gives synopsis of individual SEP's background and their responses to directed questions, concentrating on march habits and disciplines, jungle trail nets, and CT logistics. CONFIDENTIAL

SRI. <u>Interrogation of SEP, Jungle Trail Nets.</u> July 1967. Six separated enemy personnel (SEPs) were interrogated at Yala, Thailand, during July 1967 concerning CT march habits and discipline, jungle trail nets and CT logistics. Their positions and experiences while members of the Min Yuen (Peoples Movement) are described. CONFIDENTIAL

SRI. <u>Communications Systems, Thailand.</u> March 1968. Consists of working papers compiled as background for study of communications in Northeast Thailand. Describes organization, mission, operations, equipment and logistics for the following: Provincial Police, BPP; Marine Police; TNPD Air Division; Volunteer Defense Corps; Village Security Officers; Supreme Command; RTA and Signal Department; Special Operations Center; Special Forces; CSOC; CPMs; RTAF; and MDUs. Discusses target areas, village radio programs, PATs, Village Protection Teams, Board of Tax Supervision, Customs Department and ARD. Includes tambon data on Provincial Police and Village Radio Stations, and radio net maps for Kalasin, Nakhon Phanom, Nong Khai, Sakon Nakhon, Ubon Ratchathani, and Ubon Thani. CONFIDENTIAL

SRI. <u>South Thailand Border Operations Trip Report - June 1968.</u> June 1968. Reports on trip taken to gain impressions of the impact on South Thailand of the fall in rubber prices and the results of suppression operations against the CTO in Betong, Bannang Sata, Yaha, and Waeng districts. Notes lower level of consumption by small rubber holders, migrant rubber workers leaving for areas of greater employment, and employment provided by government development projects. Comments on lack of success with suppression efforts, establishment of commodity controls, and opinions on the CTO threat to Thailand. Discusses CT activity among Thai-Muslims and the relations between the RTG and the Thai-Muslims. Includes trip record and reports of interviews with cross-sections of the population. CONFIDENTIAL NOFORN

SRI. Insurgent Support Denial Measures for Southern Thailand. July 1968. Evaluates potential use of population surveillance and terrorist support denial measures as elements of a campaign to eliminate the Communist Terrorist Organization (CTO) operating along the Thai-Malaysian border. Describes ethnic structure and economy of Southern Thailand and the CTO, with reference to feasibility and application of the measures. Appraises Malayan concept of counterinsurgency in terms of its applicability to Thailand. Examines plan for separating terrorists from the people, and for regrouping the population. Makes recommendations for RTG operational planning and administrative steps. CONFIDENTIAL

SRI. Insurgency in Northeastern Thailand and Smuggling and Illegal Entry Across the Mekong River Border (U). August 1968. This report analyzes and discusses the problem of identifying and interdicting activity across the Mekong River in support of insurgents in Northeastern Thailand. An ancillary purpose was to note gaps in existing information that need to be closed in order to construct an effective system of border control. The report also attempts to set in perspective the magnitude of the subversive threat in order to infer, in very general terms, the level and trend of support requirements. These requirements include not only materiel -- such as weapons and ammunition, medical supplies and communications equipment -- but also the responsiveness of rural communities in furnishing recruits, subsistence, intelligence, and counterintelligence. CONFIDENTIAL

SRI. Status Report, PEV Border Control: Task 2, Operational Environment; Task 5, Border Area Control Subsystem. July 1968. Reports progress made toward designing a border control system for the Mekong River segment of the border. Covers insurgent logistics, present Thai security forces, socio-economic factors, and physical environment as related to border control system design. Discusses preliminary systems analyses indicating a general system concept for the land area subsystem and the requirements for tests of functional elements of this subsystem. CONFIDENTIAL NOFORN

SRI. The Logistics System of the Communist Terrorist Organization in Southern Thailand (U). July 1968. This report presents details and qualitative analyses of the Communist Terrorist (CT) logistics system in Southern Thailand. Methods of collecting money and giving support, ordering, purchase and obtaining donations of goods, transport, delivery and storage are discussed. Various methods of camp and cache detection are discussed: information from surrendered and captured enemy personnel, airborne infrared detectors, seismic detectors, the rubidium vapor magnetometer, photo reconnaissance, and others. CONFIDENTIAL

SRI. PE V, Border Control; Task 2, Operational Environment: Notes on Visits to Nong Khai and Nakhon Phanom Provinces, 24 to 2 July 1968 (CNF). August 1968. Describes the border security measures that are being enforced. Reviews the results of the issuance of Counter Subversive Operations Command (CSOC) Operational Concept No. 111 (Thai-Lao Border Area Surveillance). Evaluates the suitability of Amphoe Tha Uthen as a test area for a Border Control study. Attachments contain trip notes, a report on increased Communist terrorist activity, a chart of the Mukdahan radio network, details on Civilian-Police-Military force, and communication arrangements. A draft translation of the Gold Minute Plan is attached. CONFIDENTIAL NOFORN

SRI. An Analytic Approach to the Estimation of Counterguerrilla Capabilities (U) Draft. September 1968. This analysis is an attempt to derive indices of counterguerrilla capability for use as alternatives to the force ratio index which for years has served as a basis for regular war requirements estimates. It is part of an overall effort to estimate the forces required to defeat the Communist Terrorists (CTs) in Southern Thailand, and as such, only those strategic options that seem applicable in such a campaign are subject to detailed analysis. CONFIDENTIAL

SRI. Insurgent Logistics in Northeast Thailand. December 1968. Explains research methodology of document search, discussions with officials and interviews. Analyzes the insurgent organization and functions, covering region, district, section and groups. Discusses logistic materiel and system. Appendixes deal with group structure, locations, and relationships between insurgent organizations; movement/trail policies, support base structure, money, food, clothing, arms and ammunition, medicine, and water supply; and the issue of insurgent extortion in procuring food from the populace. CONFIDENTIAL

SRI. Security Forces and Border Control Agencies in Nakhon Phanom Province, June 1968. Describes security forces and border control agencies, and evaluates effectiveness of the organizations, regulations, and processes used in controlling the border area. Covers riverine agencies, BPP, Civil-Police-Military commands, and the RTG policy on border control. Examines civil regulations on curfews, ID systems, arms and ammunition, and aliens, drugs, and rice. Describes collation and assessment of border intelligence. Includes security forces and location in seven amphoes of Nakhon Phanom; communications networks in four border amphoes of Nakhon Phanom; and translation of RTA Operation Order No. 5 (Border Control). CONFIDENTIAL

SRI. Rice Supply and Movement of Population and Commodities in Nakhon Phanom Province. December 1968. Consists of part of the continuing study of the border control problem in Northeast Thailand. Examines major aspects of social and economic environment in Nakhon Phanom province covering supply and consumption of glutinous rice; cross-border movements of people and commodities; and the ethnic composition of population and movements of population and commodities. Analyzes implications of the rice situation and population and commodity movements for a border control system. Examines characteristics of smuggling in Nakhon Phanom and Nong Khai. CONFIDENTIAL

SRI. Communications Systems for Counterinsurgency in Northeast Thailand. February 1969. Gives results of study of the organization, missions, and operations of all forces and agencies involved in counterinsurgency operations in the Northeast, from patrol units to Bangkok headquarters. Evaluates existing communications systems and makes recommendations for improvement and development. Examines inadequacies of small-unit facilities; the complexity of joint operations; and the control of major operations by distant commands. Discusses establishment of a unified Thai National Communications Agency. Includes evaluation of ranges of manpack radios in forested areas, batteries for FM-5 radios, and message-volume capabilities. CONFIDENTIAL

SRI. Theoretical Considerations in Acoustic/Seismic Detection of Low-Flying Aircraft in Thailand. May 1969. UNCLASSIFIED

SRI. Special Project CSOC "Open Arms" Study. Reviews the background of the project dealing with the evaluation of the "Open Arms" program. Mentions difficulties experienced by Thai and US personnel in reaching an agreement on procedures to be followed. Appends memoranda, arranged chronologically, which deal with arrangements for establishing the "Open Arms" study. CONFIDENTIAL

SRI. CI Research and Analysis - Thailand, Quarterly Technical Report 2. July 1969. Examines the role of aircraft, with emphasis on rotary wing aircraft, in RTG counterinsurgency effort. Analyzes the doctrine and assumptions on which the procurement of present air capability was based, past use of aircraft in counterinsurgency, and cost/effectiveness comparisons of the study. Covers plans for air support levels analysis, system costs versus resources analysis, and manpower requirements versus resources analysis. SECRET NOFORN

SRI. Concepts for Tribal Education in Northern Thailand. August 1969. CONFIDENTIAL

SRI. An Operational Gaming Concept for Evaluation Trail Surveillance System Models in Northern Thailand. November 1969. CONFIDENTIAL

SRI. Counterinsurgency Communications. November 1969. Specifies the communication and interface requirement of multi-mix units involved in joint counterinsurgency operations. Different systems approaches to satisfy the requirement are shown and an evaluation method for selecting the most efficient system is developed. Application of the system evaluation method is shown on a practical "worth case" sample in rough mountainous terrain in Northeastern Thailand. CONFIDENTIAL NOFORN

SRI. VIST Task 1 Research Report. March 1970. Defines VIST task 1 as the Village Location and Identification file (VLIF), serving as geographic locator for the overall system. Describes the planning and analysis phase and establishment of objectives. Discusses development and documentation of work procedures and computer programs, the training of Thai personnel and testing of the system through processing data for one province. Covers procedural revisions and completion of the computerized VLIF for the Northeast. Includes information on users and future plans for the system. CONFIDENTIAL

SRI. VIST Task 2 Research Report, Vol I. March 1970. Analyzes reporting forms and techniques used by provincial officials of the RTG in NE Thailand in the collection of CT activity data. Recommends changes where needed. Notes that automated information-handling system utilizing the National Statistical Office computer was designed; programs were written and checked out; and Thai programmers and machine operators were given training in storage and retrieval of data. Mentions that a data base of approximately 9,000 reports of CT activities covering December 1965-March 1969 was established by a VIST-trained staff of Thai Information Processing Specialists working at the office of CSOC. Points out that reports and summaries from the data base were made available to RTG and US mission interested agencies. CONFIDENTIAL NOFORN

SRI. Friendly Operations Subsystem for Royal Thai Government Counterinsurgency Forces. March 1970. Defines VIST as a management information system to provide for organization, filing, and reporting of counterinsurgency information for certain interested agencies of the RTG. Contains design of a friendly operations information subsystem of VIST, along with example used of the data generated therefrom. Contends that the data, when used in conjunction with information of village locations, insurgent activities, and socioeconomic, ethnic, and geographic characteristics, will provide counterinsurgency management tools for the RTG. CONFIDENTIAL NOFORN

SRI. Analysis of Projected Staff and Budget Levels for MRDC. May 1970. FOR OFFICIAL USE ONLY

SRI. Village Information System - Thailand. July 1970. Consists of a combined research and development report by the Royal Thai Government and the US, dealing with an operational Management Information System for Thailand. Examines standardized forms developed for use in the field and computer output summaries, using English or Thai words. Mentions Thai adoption of the system, and Thai staffing, operation, and funding. Includes a village location and identification file, showing geographic and administrative contexts. CONFIDENTIAL

SRI. The Impact of RTG Assistance and Communication on Defense Related Attitude of Remote Villages.
    A. Vol 1: Village TV Study

  B. Vol II: Amphoe Phrasaeng Bulldozer Study
  C. Vol III: Methodology, Analysis, and Detailed Results
September 1970. FOR OFFICIAL USE ONLY

SRI. Annotated Index to the Data Files for the Village TV/Bulldozer Study. March 1971. FOR OFFICIAL USE ONLY

SRI. A Reference Border Control System Concept for the Thai-Lao Border (U).
  Vol I: Main Text
  Vol II: Appendices A and B, Text Results and Operational Environment
April 1971. UNCLASSIFIED

SRI. Instruction of Thai Analysts in Uses of the CI Information Center's Automated Data System. April 1971. CONFIDENTIAL

SRI. Data Review and Prototype Data Banks for the Joint Thai-US Military Research and Development Center.
  Appendix A: Administrative Code Systems
  Appendix B: Prototype Manual Data Bank Query System. Sections I-III
  Appendix B: Prototype Manual Data Bank Query System. Section IV
  Appendix C: Annotated Bibliography of MRDC/RDC-T Technical Reports
  Appendix D: Documentation for the Prototype Computerized Data Bank
  Appendix E: Relationship Between Incident Reports and Security Force Presence
August 1971. UNCLASSIFIED

SRI. Development of Demonstration Counter-Insurgency Games (Volume I, Main Text). August 1971. UNCLASSIFIED

SRI. Development of Demonstration Counter-Insurgency Games (Volume II, Appendixes). August 1971. FOR OFFICIAL USE ONLY

SRI. Task 14 - Area Communications - Field Trip to Changwats Nong Khai and Nakhon Phanom by a combined MRDC/SRI team, 11 to 17 August 1971. August 1971. CONFIDENTIAL

SRI. Village Information Systems-Thailand. August 1971. CONFIDENTIAL

SRI. Preliminary Statistics on Scientific and Technological Potential of Thailand. December 1971. UNCLASSIFIED

SRI. MACTHAI/AFAG Problem Definition Study: RTAF Night Operations. May 1972. CONFIDENTIAL

SRI. Programs Definition of an Improved Resource Management Systems for the Royal Thai Armed Forces. August 1972. UNCLASSIFIED

SRI. <u>RTAF C-47 Gunship Night Augmentation (MACTHAI/AFAG Problem Definition Study: RTAF Night Operations 23 May 1972)</u>. August 1972. CONFIDENTIAL

SRI. <u>Programs Definition of an Improved Financial Management Systems for the Royal Thai Army</u>. September 1972. UNCLASSIFIED

Thailand Information Center (TIC). <u>The Mekong River</u> (An Annotated Bibliography). March 1967. UNCLASSIFIED

TIC. <u>Bibliography on Shan</u>. No date. UNCLASSIFIED

TIC. <u>Bibliography on Lisu</u>. No date. UNCLASSIFIED

TIC. <u>Bibliography on the Vietnamese in Thailand</u>. October 1970. UNCLASSIFIED

TIC. <u>Bibliography on Government and Politics in Thailand at the National Level</u>. October 1970. UNCLASSIFIED

TIC. <u>Bibliography on Government and Politics in Thailand at the Changwat Level</u>. October 1970. UNCLASSIFIED

TIC. Bibliography on Government and Politics in Thailand at the Amphoe, Tambon, and Muban Level with a Supplement on the Bangkok-Thonburi Metropolitan Area. October 1970. UNCLASSIFIED

TIC. <u>Bibliography on Narcotics</u>. April 1971. UNCLASSIFIED

TIC. <u>List of Journals Published in Thailand</u>. September 1971. UNCLASSIFIED

TIC. Specialists on the Hill Tribes of Thailand. December 1971. UNCLASSIFIED

Royal Thai Government (RTG) Ministry of Defense/Supreme Command Headquarters. Financial Manual re Thai Government Officials' Salary Scale and Per-diem Allowances. (English translation). 1964. Contains schedules of salary and per-diem allowances by rank and position of commissioned and non-commissioned officers, civilian employees, police officers, and judicial and executive officials. Classifies special travel allowances and special per-diem allowances of government officials for traveling in Thailand and abroad. Budgetary policy for social entertainment, scholarships and other expenditures are described. Presents diagrams showing military budget for FY 1960 - 1963 for each division of the Royal Thai Army, Navy, Air Force, and Supreme Command Headquarters. CONFIDENTIAL

RTG, Royal Thai Army/CPM 1. <u>The Communist Terrorists in the Northeastern Thailand</u>. October 1967. Gives historical background of communist terrorists (CTs) operating in Thailand, including statements of villagers trained abroad. Presents plans, concepts, and operations of CTs. Defines CT areas and lists incidents to March, 1967. Defines the stages of CT operations. Describes activities, divisions, groupings and locations, tactics and arms of CTs. Includes stories about specific incidents and identifies some characteristics and traits as well as deception and security measures. Discusses type of support the CTs receive from abroad, including propaganda, money, arms, and food. Describes CT methods of storing food supplies and their actual living conditions. CONFIDENTIAL

RTG, Ministry of National Development/National Energy Authority. Survey of Thailand Power Equipment, Final Report. December 1964. Surveys natural energy resources, both water power potential and fossil fuels. Considers demography, electric energy consumption, electrical installations, and equipment to be built. Investigates economic aspects of the project. Includes a correlation between electric energy consumption and national income as well as an investment and replacement scheme. Includes graphs and charts made during the survey. RESTRICTED (CONFIDENTIAL)

Pornkaew, Saisit (Translated from Thai by Osborn, George K., III). Winning the War in the Villages and Defeating the Terrorists: A Thai View, US Army War College/Carlisle Barracks-Student Thesis. March 1970. FOR OFFICIAL USE ONLY

United States Government (US Govt). Various Reports, Airgrams, and Miscellaneous Documents. Bangkok: American Embassy. Through May 1973. A sampling of documents recorded on CHECO microfilm cartridges, SECRET NOFORN 875-78. American Embassy Development and Security selected CI files and card catelog of the SRI field office filmed 8-11 June 1973. The overall classification of these documents is SECRET NOFORN

US Govt, Department of the Navy/Officer in Charge of Construction (OICC). Chiengmai Medical School Hospital. July 1966. Consists of a letter to the deputy director of USOM with regard to construction problems on the site of the Chieng Mai Medical School Hospital. Explains compromises, concessions, disagreements, and misunderstandings between OICC and the contractor. Mentions difficulties of administering a contract under the committee system. UNCLASSIFIED

US Govt, HQ USMACTHAI/JUSMAGTHAI. Country Logistics Improvement Plan. December 1971. CONFIDENTIAL

US Govt, HQ USMACTHAI/JUSMAGTHAI. Mekong River Crossing Site Study. April 1967. CONFIDENTIAL

US Govt, HQ USMACTHAI/JUSMAGTHAI. JUSMAGTHAI Support for RTN Mekong River Project. July 1971. CONFIDENTIAL NOFORN

US Govt, USMACT/JUSMAGT. RTARF Employment in the Northeast. June 1967. Evaluates Royal Thai Armed Forces (RTARF) employment in Northeast Thailand in support of Royal Thai Government counterinsurgency programs, and identifies areas in which improvements in RTARF employment are possible. Available incident statistics are examined in an effort to assess the efficiency and success of RTARF elements. Functions and roles of the Royal Thai Army, Royal Thai Air Force, Volunteer Defense Corps, Thai National Police Department, and Communist Suppression Operations Command in the overall counterinsurgency picture are examined and discussed. CONFIDENTIAL

US Govt, USMACT/JUSMAGT. The Hill Tribes Problem. February 1968. The hill tribes security force personnel are evaluated. The loyalty of hill tribes policemen is considered, as is credibility among the tribes on RTG concern for them. Possible solutions to the hill tribes problem, including ethnic minority governments and integration into the national community, are analyzed. Suggestions are made for improvement of RTG border forces. Concept and capability of 46th SFCA Support of RTG internal security operations in hill tribe areas are discussed. Costs of equipment for 46th Special Forces Company (Airborne) are listed. CONFIDENTIAL

US Govt, American Embassy. Financial Resources and Priorities in Thailand, 1967-70. April 1968. Discusses RTG budgets from 1962-71, noting shift in emphasis to development expenditures. Considers impact of US programs on RTG budgets. Suggests desirable additional expenditures for military personnel, operations, training and logistics, and maintenance and operation of equipment supplied under the Military Assistance Program (MAP). Examines the economic consequences of additional expenditures in the RTG budget. Makes recommendations regarding counterinsurgency, development, and the military. Includes analysis of MAP-Ministry of Defense (MOD) budget interactions and a rationale for US aid to Thailand. CONFIDENTIAL

US Govt, American Embassy: Communist Suppression Operation Command (CSOC). Royal Thai Government (RTG) 0910 Plan. July 1967. Lists Village Security forces by target area, showing Muban (village) names, map coordinates, strength of security force, and strike unit. Contains a list of incidents by target area considered serious from CSOC's point of view and the PAT/CA locations and strengths as of May 31, 1967. CONFIDENTIAL

US Govt, National Security Council; AID. The Implications of Thai Bureaucratic Policy for U.S. Assistance Strategy. November 1969. Analyzes Thai bureaucratic policy and summarized basic features of the Thai decision-making process. Identifies major factions and groups and principle interests and objectives of Thai leaders. Examines the importance of personal relationships to decision making and compares this to the role of institutional rivalry. Evaluates recent trends in bureaucratic power and influence. Discusses the US role as a catalyst and innovator of new programs and suggests alternate scenarios for Thai political change. Studies differences in Thai and US priorities and objectives, and problems of Thai political stability in the 1970s. Recommends changes in US advsiory and training inputs to bring the programs into closer accord with Thai political realities. SECRET NOFORN

US Govt, Department of State; AID/Office of Public Safety. Assessment and Development Plans, Thai National Police Department, Aviation Division. September 1968. Assesses the Aviation Division organization, mission and performance to plan for development of the Division as police air lift support for counterinsurgency. Makes recommendations regarding the organization, operations, aircraft equipment and facilities, maintenance and logistics, contract assistance, ground and flight safety program, management, communications capability, and budgeting. Comments on lack of RTG approval of the Aviation Division and the Division's links with the Border Patrol Police. Describes helicopter pilot training for the Division. Maps show aircraft deployment and location of tambon stations. CONFIDENTIAL

US Govt, American Embassy. Unidentified Aircraft Intruding into Thailand's Airspace. June 1967. CONFIDENTIAL NOFORN

US Govt, American Embassy (CINCPAC). Study of Intrusions into Thailand Airspace (U). December 1967. CONFIDENTIAL NOFORN LIMDIS

US Govt, American Embassy Bangkok. Organization of Counter-Insurgency Operations in Northeastern Thailand Under Second Army. January 1968. Describes organization and function of CSOC (Communist Suppression Operations Center). Reports on organization of Second Army Forward. Contains charts. CONFIDENTIAL

US Govt, American Embassy Bangkok. Roles and Missions of RTG and US Forces and Agencies in Base Defense Operations. May 1968. CONFIDENTIAL NOFORN

US Govt, American Embassy Bangkok. Insurgency Situation North Thailand. February 1969. CONFIDENTIAL

GLOSSARY OF ABBREVIATIONS AND ACRONYMS*

A.	Amphoe (district)
AFG	Amphoe Farmers Group
AFIOC	Armed Forces Intelligence Operations Center
AFSC	Armed Forces Security Center
AID	Agency for International Development
AIO	Assistant Information Officer
AOC	Air Operations Center
APC	Armored Personnel Carrier
ARD	Accelerated Rural Development
ARL	Aerial Reconnaissance Laboratory
ARPA	Advanced Research Projects Agency
ASEAN	Association of Southeast Asian Nations
B.	Ban (village)
BAC	Bank for Agriculture and Agricultural Cooperatives
BCP	Border Control Points
B.E.	Buddhist Era
BIC	Border Information Center (Border Patrol Police)
BOB	Bureau of the Budget
BPAO	Branch Public Affairs Officer (USIS)
BPP	Border Patrol Police
BSVT	Border Security Volunteer Team
C.	Changwat (province)
CA	Census Aspiration
CAC	Civic Actions Center
CAO	Cultural Affairs Officer
CAP	Country Assistance Program
CCARD	Coordinating Committee of Accelerated Rural Development (Central Committee of Accelerated Rural Development)
CCOP	Committee for Coordination and Operational Planning
CCP	Chinese Communist Party
CCPT	Chinese Communist Party of Thailand
CD	Community Development
CDTC	Combat Development Test Center
CHJUSMAG	Chief, Joint United States Military Assistance Group
CI	Counterinsurgency
CIA	Central Intelligence Agency
CIB	Central Investigation Bureau
CID	Criminal Investigation Division
CINCPAC	Commander in Chief, Pacific
CINCPACFLT	Commander in Chief, Pacific Fleet
COMUSMACTHAI	Commander, US Military Assistance Command, Thailand

---

*Not all of these acronyms and abbreviations appear in this report. However, they do appear widely in the literature that the reader may want to consult.

CPAO	Country Public Affairs Officer
CPM	Comm-Party of Malaya/Malaysia, Civilian-Police-Military
CPR	Chinese People's Republic
CPS	Communist Party of Siam
CPT	Communist Party of Thailand
CSC	Communist Suppression Committee
CSMC	CI Support Management Center
CSOC	Communist Suppression Operations Center (or Command)
CSOD	Communist Prevention and Suppression Directorate
CSOR	Communist Suppression Operations Region
CT	Communist Terrorist
CTO	Communist Terrorist Organization
DASC	Direct Air Support Center
DDP	Developing Democracy Program
DH	direct hire
DOA	Department of Agriculture
DOH	Department of Health
DOLA	Department of Local Administration
DRV	Democratic Republic of Vietnam
DS	Development and Security
DTEC	Department of Technical and Economic Cooperation
ECAFE	Economic Commission for Asia and the Far East
FAC	Forward Air Controller
FAO	Food and Agriculture Organization
FAR	Forces Armees de Royale (Royal Laotian Army)
FLA	Farmers Liberation Association
FY	fiscal year
GED	General Education Development
GRC	Government of the Republic of China
GVN	Government of Vietnam
HPP	Highway Patrol Police
HTV	Hill-Tribe Volunteers
IA	Information Assistant
I/CI	Insurgency/Counterinsurgency
ISAC	Internal Security Analysis Section
ISP	Internal Security Plan
ISUMS	Incident Summaries
JSC	Joint Security Center
JST	Joint Security Team
K.A.	King Amphoe
KIA	Killed In Action
KMT	Kuomintang

LDP	Lao Dong Party
LMG	Light Machinegun
LP	Line Platoon
LRRP	Long Range Reconnaissance Patrol
MAAG	Military Assistance and Advisory Group
MACTHAI	Military Assistance Command, Thailand
MACTHAI/ JUSMAGTHAI	Military Assistance Command, Thailand/ Joint US Military Assistance Group, Thailand
MAP	Military Assistance Program
MAVU	Mobile Audio Visual Unit
MCA	Military Civic Actions
MCP	Malaysian Communist Party
MCYL	Malaysian Communist Youth League
MDU	Mobile Development Unit
MDU/CC	Mobile Development Unit Construction Company
MEDCAP	Medical Civic Action Program
MIST	Mobile Information Service Team
MIT	Mobile Information Team
MLP	Mobile Line Platoon
MMT	Mobile Medical Team
MOA	Ministry of Agriculture
MOD	Ministry of Defense
MOE	Ministry of Education
MOI	Ministry of Interior
MOND	Ministry of National Development
MOPH	Ministry of Public Health
MP	Member of Parliament
MRDC	Military Research and Development Center
MRP	Mobile Reserve Platoon
MTT	Mobile Training Team
MTTS	Mobile Trade Training Schools
MTTU	Mobile Trade Training Unit
MVT	Model Village Team
NCA (NCNA)	New China News Agency
NCO	Noncommissioned Officer
NEA	National Energy Authority
NEARDC	Northeast ARD Center
NEDB	National Economic Development Board
NEEA	Northeast Electric Authority
NEED	Northeast Economic Development
NETI	Northeast Technical Institute
NIDA	National Institute of Development Administration
NIPSO	National Information and Psychological Operations Organization
NLA	National Liberation Association
NLO	National Liberation Organization
NLHS	Neo Lao Hak Sat

NRC	National Research Center
NSC	National Security Command
NSCC	National Security Command Center
NSO	National Statistic Office
NVA	North Vietnamese Army
NVN	North Vietnam
OPM	Office of the Prime Minister
OPVA	Overseas Patriotric Vietnamese Association
OSD	Office of the Secretary of Defense
PAD	Police Air Division
PAR	Project Appraisal Report
PARU	Police Aerial Reinforcement Unit
PAS	United Muslim Party of the Golden Peninsula
PASA	Participating Agency Service Agreement
PAT	People's Assistance Team
PEA	Provincial Electric Authority
PFF	Police Field Force
PFT	Patriotic Front of Thailand
PIPS	Project implementation plan
PL	Pathet Lao
PLA	People's Liberation Army
PLIM	Pan Malaya Islamic Movement
POMIL	Political-Military
PP	Provincial Police
PRD	Public Relations Department
ProAg	Program Agreement
PROP	project proposal
PSYOPS	Psychological Operations
RAC	Research Analysis Corporation
RAS	Remote Area Security
RASD	Remote Area Security Development
RCT	Regimental Combat Team
RDFU	Research and Development Field Unit
RDTE	Research, Development, Testing, and Evaluation
RLG	Royal Lao Government
RP	Railway Police
RSSP	Rural Security Systems Program
RTA	Royal Thai Army
RTAF	Royal Thai Air Force
RTARF	Royal Thai Armed Forces
RTASF	Royal Thai Army Special Forces
RTAVF	Royal Thai Army Volunteer Force
RTAVN	Royal Thai Army-Vietnam
RTG	Royal Thai Government
RTMC	Royal Thai Marine Corps
RTN	Royal Thai Navy

SA	Special Assistant
SA/CI	Special Assistant for Counterinsurgency
SAF	Special Action Force
SB	Special Branch
SEAMEO	Southeast Asian Ministers of Education Organization
SEATO	Southeast Asia
SLFPA	Self Liberated Farmers & Planters Association
SOC	Special Operations Center
SRI	Stanford Research Institute
SRT	State Railways of Thailand
SSB	single-side-band
SSP	South Seas Party
STEM	Special Technical and Economic Mission
STOL	Short-Takeoff-and-Landing
T.	Tambon
TAAG	Thailand Army Advisory Group
TACS	Tactical Air Control System
TACP	Tactical Air Control Parties
TAFAG	Thailand Air Force Advisory Group
TAOR	Tactical Area of Operational Responsibility
TCP	Thai Communist Party
TDC	Tambon Development Committee
TFPW	Thailand Federation of Patriotic Workers
TFY	Thai fiscal year
TIC	Thailand Information Center
TIM	Thai Independence Movement
TNAG	Thailand Navy Advisory Group
TNPD	Thai National Police Department
TOC	Tactical Operations Center
TOE	Table of Organization and Equipment
TPF	Thailand Patriotic Front
TPLAF	Thai People's Liberation Armed Forces
TPYO	Thailand Patriotic Youth Organization
TUFEC	Thai-UNESCO Fundamental Education Center
UN	United Nations
UNDP	United Nations Development Program
UNESCO	United Nations Educational, Scientific, & Cultural Organization
UNICEF	United Nations International Children's Emergency Fund
UNSF	United Nations Special Fund
US	United States
USA	United States Army
USAF	United States Air Force
USARPAC	US Army-Pacific
USARSUPTHAI	US Army Support-Thailand
USASF	US Army Special Forces
USIA	US Information Agency

USIS	US Information Service
USOM	United States Operations Mission
USSR	Union of Soviet Socialist Republics (Soviet Union)
VDC	Volunteer Defense Corps
VDD	Volunteer Defense Division
VHS	Village Health and Sanitation
VIST	Village Security Information System
VLO	Volunteer Liberation Organization
VOPT	Voice of the People of Thailand
VPT	Village Protection Team
VPU	Village Protection Unit
VRS	Village Radio System
VSDU	Village Security and Development Unit
VSF	Village Security Force
VSO	Village Security Officer
VST	Village Security Teams
WAY	Women and Youth Program
WHO	World Health Organization
WIA	Wounded in Action
WWII	World War II

GLOSSARY OF TERMS

Amphoe	Administrative division of a changwat; comparable to a county.
Baht	Thai unit of currency; one baht (₿1.00) is approximately equivalent to US$.05.
Changwat	The principal administrative division of Thailand; comparable to a province or state.
Kamnan	Appointed (or in some cases elected) head of a tambon.
King Amphoe	A sub-amphoe established when the increasing population of an amphoe or the security situation warrants more decentralized control.
Mathayom	Thai secondary school formerly consisting of eight grades following four years of primary school; currently consists of five grades following seven years of primary school.
Muban	Village.
Nai Amphoe	Appointed head of an amphoe.
Palad Amphoe	Deputy to a nai amphoe.
Palad Changwat	Deputy to a changwat governor; usually more than one, each with a separate function.
Phuyaiban	Elected chief of a village.
Prathom	Thai elementary school formerly consisting of four grades; currently consisting of seven grades.
Tambon	Administrative division of an amphoe; comparable to a township.
Sapha Tambon	Tambon council.
Wat	An enclosed area containing the buildings associated with Buddhist worship; the temple compound (usually one in every village).